JUST ANOTHER ORDINARY LIFE

Written by life and Miroslav (Mirek) Kolias

© 2021 Miroslav Kolias. All rights reserved. No part of this publication may be reproduced, distributed, or transmitted in any form or by any means, including photocopying, recording, or other electronic or mechanical methods, without the prior written permission of the publisher, except in the case of brief quotations embodied in critical reviews and certain other noncommercial uses permitted by copyright law. ISBN: 978-1-66781-865-8

THANK YOU, DAD, for taking the time to gather your memories and put them on paper for all of us to enjoy, share, and marvel over. The many generations (hopefully) to come will be appreciative of the time and dedication you have put into this project. Your life, and our family's, has been anything but ordinary. I am so glad you and Mom found each other in all the turmoil and found peace and love together.

Contents

The beginning. 1
Under Nazi occupation. 6
The end of war. 16
To Liberec 23
The second beginning. 30
Under the Communist regime. 38
The apprenticeship years. 45
The dark day. 51
Coping. 55
After graduating. 61
In the Army. 69
A coal mining soldier. 79
Marta. 90
The third beginning. 103
Milena. 113
Is the real Spring really coming? 122
September 21 1968. 130
Hopeful good-bye. 133
Waiting in Austria. 137
The fourth beginning. 150
Horner Street, Union City. 159
To Sleepy Hollow. 169
The last (?) beginning. 175
Building our future. 183
Moving on. 197
Epilogue. 203
Marta's last days 205

The beginning.

On April 26, 1945 I turned to be nine.

Boy, Mirek, has it really been 61years since then?!

Two weeks later The War in Europe ended. Not that my turning nine would have anything to do with the end of war. This monumental event had a profound impact on our whole family, though. The end of war, I mean.

About a month earlier my mother would, on a foot propelled sewing machine, sew a large Yugoslavian flag from white, red and blue pieces of cloth cut from different garments. This was not a simple matter. If anyone would see that and report it to the German authorities, our whole family would end up in a concentration camp with the most dire consequences. My brother Pavel, five at that time, and I were sworn to secrecy, and I am proud to say that we did adhere to the promise despite the many temptations to reveal this secret to our many play-friends.

At that time my family used to live in a small village Circe adjacent to a larger town Kranj in Slovenia, part of then called Yugoslavia.

Miroslav Kolias

My father Antonin (called Tonda) was twenty years old when summoned by his father Josef to come there from Czechoslovakia after the promised job of a production manager of a large textile factory in Kranj did not pan out. When my grandfather came to introduce himself to the owner of the mill, he was greeted with an incredulous: "Mr. Kolias, do you know what day this is?" My grandfather, replying in negative, was told that it was Friday the 13th, and that because of that, he couldn't, unfortunately, be hired as promised!

Grandfather Josef was, of course, devastated. He has sold all family belongings in Czechoslovakia and left for Slovenia with his wife Ruzena and family to follow as soon as he established himself there. Being of a tough and resourceful breed he started to look around for some other opportunity to earn living. As it was, nobody needed a textile print technician right then.

Finally, he found an old, closed down hide processing plant for rent. After inspecting it he concluded that it could be turned into a small dye house. That's when he called my father and my uncle Josef (called Pepa) to stop their studies, and come to help him to build a new future in Kranj, Slovenia. Beside my father and uncle Pepa there were also my uncle Zdenek, the oldest, and aunt Ella. They both were already married and had their own families in Czechoslovakia, where they remained.

So it happened that the three of them, with much difficulties, started a business dyeing and re-dyeing peoples clothes, and later on even small lots of fabric and yarn for many local, established textile mills. The plant was a very primitive one, everything had to be done by hand, and even heating up water in vats was achieved by building fire under them. After a few years of very hard, and time consuming, work they were able to buy a piece of land on the shores of river Sava, borrow additional money and build a new, modern textile plant just few years before the start of World War II.

Kranj, being a textile industry town, had a vibrant Czech community (because the Czech textile industry was world known, so Czech technicians were widely sought after) whose members were actively participating in all kinds of social activities. Several Czech clubs were formed. Amongst those would be SOKOL, a group concentrating on ethnic preservation, collective exercises, children's activities and so on.

Prominent member of SOKOL was also Marek's family. Antonin Marek worked as a textile plant superintendent in a different mill than the one Josef Kolias was originally offered a job. Antonin Marek and his wife Anna have had three pretty daughters, Milena, Bozena (Bozka) and Jaroslava (Jara) of which Milena was the oldest, some eighteen years of age then and learning to be a seamstress.

As it happened, on one of the Czech social gatherings my future father and mother Milena found an attraction for each other. They both liked to dance, touring the country and climb Slovenia's abundant and beautiful mountains. After about two years of dating, in February 1935, they decided to get married, just about at the same time the new plant was being finished.

My father was of Catholic religion while my mother was a Czech Brothers, a protestant denomination follower. My mother did not have any objections in changing her religion to my fathers as there were no Czech Brothers in Slovenia. When they approached the local Catholic Priest with the idea, they were told that they would have to attend some schooling in Catholic faith lasting about six months. Being in love and impatient that seemed to be a long time to wait. The other most popular religion in Slovenia was Russian Orthodox, so they both decided to convert to it. An Orthodox Pop they visited with their request, surprisingly told them that there is no problem with that, and after they paid some fees he pronounced them to be of Orthodox faith on the spot. That's how I, born fourteen months later, and my brother Pavel, born in 1939, became of Orthodox faith.

That is probably why our family never was very religious. We just tried to live our lives in Christian principles having the Ten Commandments as our guiding credo.

Both my parents worked hard in the new Josef Kolias and Sons mill which consisted of a weaving plant under my uncle Pepa's supervision, and the bleaching, dyeing and printing plant under my father's supervision. My grandfather Josef was in charge of finances. The mill was built with well advanced technology, mechanized machinery, high pressure steam source for heating water, and so on.

To start another textile mill in the town full of textile mills is not an easy task. As I was told, the family had a very hard time to get the mill off the ground and to become a prosperous one. The whole mill at its peak employed about 60 people, and between the payroll and the loan payments there was not much left for another three (my uncle Pepa married another Czech girl Bozena Neumannova) families to live on.

I remember in all those years being on a family vacation only once, a week by the Mediterranean Sea on a little island named Krk (Neck in translation). And I was afraid of water, my mom tells me......

I was born in an apartment rented by my parents in a nice Kranj neighborhood Na Planinah, where Pavel was also born three and half years later. Between the two of us my mother had an unfortunate miscarriage of a baby girl after seeing the original movie Frankenstein which have upset her very much. Since it happened fairly late in her pregnancy, the whole family was very concerned that she might not be able to have another baby, but, fortunately, Pavel's arrival proved otherwise.

I do not, of course, remember much of my first four years of life, except that in our front garden there was a large rhubarb plant whose stalks I loved to peel and eat. I guess I always liked sour tasting things. I remember liking to chew on sour grass growing on the road embankments, and my mother telling me not to do it "because the sour taste comes from all the frogs peeing on it." Her warnings didn't change a thing, though.

Clockwise from the top:

My parents' wedding photo, 1935.
Grandfather Marek, aunt Jara and I, 1938.
Pavel and I, 1944.
The factory, 1940.
The house in Circe, 1940.
Mom after grandpa Marek's death, 1944
Grandma Marek, aunts Jara, Bozka, mom, 1943.
Grandpa Kolias, my father, uncle Pepa, 1938.

Under Nazi occupation.

In 1940 Yugoslavia was occupied by German forces, and all the younger men of Czech origin were taken and put in prison to make sure that they would not help local resistance against the occupation. My father was one of them.

My grandfather Marek was also taken, but instead in prison like the others, he was put in a concentration camp, under much much harsher conditions. The reason behind it was that at the time when the Nazi Party and Hitler came to power in Germany, one of my grandfather's friends, a German, joined the Nazi party, too. They both were part of a group who played marionet theater for kids. At that time my grandfather asked him how he could have joined the Nazi Party, doesn't he see where it all is leading to? And he added: "We have been friends for many years, and I like you, but I hate your decision to become a member of the Nazi Party." This was sufficient for my grandfather Marek being imprisoned in the concentration camp where he died of hunger later on. My father was fortunately released in about two months, after being thoroughly and brutally interrogated, as were the other Czech men.

My maternal grandmother, who we all affectionately called Babka, and her two unmarried daughters Bozka and Jara were taken into Germany to be the forced laborers there. They were allowed to take only the minimum of their clothes with them and were transported to a large house in Starenberg, ten people to a room. Both my aunts were working in Munich as housemaids in the households of some prominent Nazi Party members. Over the week they would stay with their masters, and after 16 hours of daily work they would get to sleep in a damp and cold cellar. Both aunts got terrible rheumatoid arthritis there and suffered with it for the rest of their lives. Babka did some menial work around the camp. All of them worked for free, of course.

When my father was imprisoned, my mother with the two of us kids, moved into house that belonged to the mill, and stayed there even after my father came home from his imprisonment. The house was built on a large, slopey ground overlooking the factory. It had a basement and two floors that were occupied by my grandparents and my uncle Pepa with aunt Bozena, who we called Boza. In order to accommodate us, uncle and aunt moved with my grandparents, and we got the upper floor for ourselves. The house was built as a single-family home, so the top two floors were interconnected by a wide stairway with massive railings that served to Pavel and me as grand toboggans. Our floor consisted of a kitchen, two bedrooms, a hallway and a toilet. There also was a large open balcony overlooking the wide valley in which the factory stood. Behind the mill river Sava was visible running briskly under the opposite side of the valley. Above the river, in the middle of the valley side there was a railroad track built into it.

Many times, especially toward the end of war, standing on the balcony Pavel and I would watch in amazement Allied aircrafts striking, with great noise, right over our heads and shooting at the engine pulling military supply trains. When the engine was hit, compressed steam started to escape, whistling loudly. What a show! We would always marvel over the precision of the attack, and how those pilots, after shooting at the engines, were able to move their crafts straight up without hitting the opposite side of the valley.

I remember that one time we got a permission to visit Babka and my aunts at their camp in Germany. My parents and I (Pavel was still too small for such a journey) went by train to Austria, and continued by an electric train through a beautiful mountainous country into Germany. It was my first time on an electric train, and I liked it very much. The quiet, clean train was so much different from the noisy, smoke and steam belching one we just arrived on. We got a room by the large Starnberg Lake, close to the town Starnberg. As we were coming to our hotel in pitch dark night (during the war much of the country had to be in total darkness at night because of the air raids) we saw several bright searchlights combing the sky, searching for eventual Allied aircrafts. I liked that, but to my parents it was an ominous show.

Next day, it had to be the week-end, we were allowed to enter Babka's room. It was a large, high-ceilinged room crammed with double cots with dark grey blankets on them. Babka and both aunts greeted us profusely, and everybody started to cry. Later on Babka explained to us, that it's preferable to have the bottom cot, as the ever present bedbugs would get on the ceiling, and would let themselves drop down on the sleeping people below.

"Why don't they just crawl from the floor up?" I wanted to know, after which Babka pointed to the cot legs each ending in a can filled up with water to prevent just that.

"And where do you take your bath?" I asked when noticing the absence of any washing facility in the room.

"Well", aunt Bozka answered, "you just have to spit way high, and as the spit comes down, you jump right through it!" Little did I know that a camp like this was actually a luxurious one. People were not tortured and killed in the ones housing the forced laborers, opposite to those exterminating concentration camps, where people were sent to be killed at the end.

We were allowed to spend the whole day together, and even were able to get out and have a picnic in a meadow under a large monument to Bismarck, a late German chancellor.

After returning from our trip to Germany I was supposed to attend the first grade school. Since my mother didn't want me to go to a German run school, she enlisted me to a private one, where a Slovenia lady teacher would teach me for almost three full years. It was not allowed to do anything like that, but my mother was never too keen on following some, unacceptable to her, rules.

When the Allied started to pressure German army on many fronts, our mill was forced to transform to a large cleaning and washing station. German soldiers, returning from the front, were brought to specially build chambers to be thoroughly washed and cleansed of all pests. Their uniforms, often torn and bloodied, would also be washed and returned back to the Army. As it was very difficult to keep tab on the thousands of garments and blankets throughout the whole process, my parents were able to sneak some of them away, and deliver them to the starving and needy resistant fighters, called "partisans", in the hills.

My mother had built a net of reliable people, who acted as contacts with partisans. Of course, all that was punishable by shooting death. That wouldn't deter my parents, though.

I remember one beautiful day taking a trip into the mountains with my parents. When we climbed this steep hill, and were all by ourselves, a young man appeared suddenly. My father and I continued walking. My mother stopped and conversed with this not very appealingly looking man for quite some time. After she joined us again, there was no talking about what has happened, but I was sure that the man was a Partisan. Few days after this a Partisan died delivering a bomb to the occupational city office. The bomb exploded prematurely while the man was still on his bicycle. It was not so, but I always imagined that it was the same man we met. I felt very sorry for him.

The situation in occupied Yugoslavia was a complicated one. Croatia, part of Yugoslavia always wanted to be an independent state. As it happened, lots of Croats actually sympathized with Germans as they hoped to fulfill their long standing dream of independence through them. Croatian militia, called Ustasa was formed and was operating alongside regular German occupying forces. The Partisans, under Josip Broz Tito, operated guerrilla war by attacking suddenly German Army convoys and other targets. After each attack they escaped into the hills and mountains, where because of vast popular help, were safe. Many German expeditions into the mountains to dislodge Partisans failed to achieve their goal.

After each Partisan attack, the occupying forces took a revenge on civilian population, though. People living in the high country would be gathered as suspect of aiding Partisans and taken away to Germany. Few times even happened that they would be put and locked in a wooden barn which would, consequently, be burned down to ground.

Even in occupied Czechoslovakia, after in England trained group was smuggled into the country and assassinated top German official K. H. Frank, the whole village of Lidice near Prague was completely decimated, all men and women shot and kids taken to Germany for "re-education".

In the meantime, Pavel and I were oblivious to the perils of war. We would be out and away all day if possible, running with the local kids, bathing in the Sava river, and generally causing some mischief. When she couldn't stand it any more, my mother would spank us with her cooking wooden spoons. No, she wouldn't go too far for them. Yes, our mother had us kids on a pretty short leash, but we never felt any lack of love for us from both of our parents. When we got punishment, it was always explained to us in calm voices, no shouting, and we accepted it knowing that we deserved it.

I remember one incident particularly. Since the house did not have a built in bathtub nor a shower (something I now find very strange), three times a week we would go down to the mill after 5 PM, when the operations there ceased, for bathing in one of the clean vats. First the two of us, our parents afterwards. Since the vats were very large, industrial ones, there was no need to exchange water in them after we finished. There wouldn't be enough hot water to fill them

up again anyway, as the boiler room was already shut down. I don't remember the reason for my action, but after Pavel and I finished our bath, I pulled the plug letting all the water out! When our parents came to take their bath, there was no hot water left for them. Obviously, my behind felt the consequences. On the top of it, which I always hated the most, I got a stern lecture about good and bad behavior, together with my mom's tears of sadness. I felt very rotten indeed.

For protecting the mill against burglars at night, there were two large dogs there, running on long chains attached to long cables alongside the factory walls. Pavel had no fear of the dogs. When my mother would try to catch and punish him, he would run into one of the dog's cages and call to her: "OK, come and get me!" Unfortunately, he had to get home eventually, so the spanking would be in case like that double harsh. In the winter time, too, we would have the dogs pull our sled, which was very exhilarating to us.

Winter was a fun time for us, kids. Slovenia have quite severe and long lasting winters with lots of snow. That suited us very well. Being dressed warmly with hats covering our ears and gloves protecting our hands we would play outside all day long, building snow men, making "angels" and waging great snowball wars with the local boys.

Christmas was always a special time for us. Christmas is celebrated very differently in Slovenia and in the Czech Republic. Christmas trees would be purchased only one or two days prior to Christmas Eve. Our parents would select one room, mostly the living room, to put the Christmas tree in without our knowledge. The room would be kept locked, so we, the kids, could not get in it. After we would go to sleep, our parents would decorate the tree with chocolates especially wrapped in colorful glittering wrappings and hanging on strings. Only few ornaments would be used. Mostly it was chocolates and especially for that purpose home-made flat cookies with hanging hooks attached. The whole tree was than adorned with lots of hanging sparklers and at the tip of every branch a small, colorful candle was attached.

On Christmas Eve, after our breakfast we could not eat anything until the festive dinner consisting of breaded carp and potato salad, with lots of goodies following. The reason for not eating was that we could see the Golden Piglet flying around outside. After dinner our father would take us, kids, outside to look. He would have a flashlight hidden in his coat sleeve, and at the right moment flash it over the tips of trees or roofs of houses.

"Golden piglet! Golden piglet!" we would shout, and were glad that we did not eat anything and miss the spectacle. OK, I know, I know....

Anyway, after that we would head home, and just as we would open the door, a crystal bell would ring. While we were outside, our mother would bring the gifts in the locked room and placed them under the tree. She would be spying us through a window, and when given some signal by our father outside, started to lit the candles and sparklers on. When entering the house, she would ring the bell. "What was that? What was that?" we would ask, our hearts excited. "I think it was Baby Jesus bringing the tree" our mom would answer, and we would all rush to the "secret" room. After opening its door, we would be rewarded with this awesome sight at the magnificent Christmas tree all ablaze in the sparklers and candles. We would stand still for a minute, taking it all in. Then our attention shifted to the gifts under the tree. There wouldn't be many of them. Usually, it would be one main gift for each member of the family, and only few smaller ones. I have to add that books were always given.

The mill also owned a horse, a creamy white with black patches on. It was used to pull a wagon with finished goods to be delivered to our customers, and pick fresh orders up. The horse Riza was also a great friend of ours. Many times we would ride it without a saddle or blanket under our butts.

Living in the country was great. Pavel and I loved to run around without any shoes. In the spring, we could not wait when we would be able to do that. My mother would always say: "You have to wait until the trees have the first green leaves". Of course, we were on a lookout for any tiny green thing to appear on a branch and bring it home with demands of being allowed to run around barefooted.

I have to confess, though, that not always I was happy with Pavel being around. Both our parents working in the mill, I was in charge of him, and many times, when he did something that was a no-no, I was blamed for it: "You are the older one, you have to prevent that!" And the wooden spoon would come out of its drawer. One day my mother came home from work and was looking for Pavel. He was not there.

"Mirek, where is Pavel"? she demanded, and I could not answer that. We both ran out, looking for him. He was nowhere to be seen. We went down to the factory, into the village - still no Pavel. After returning home, I had to go to the bathroom, and there he was! Sleeping as a baby on the potty! To be fair this time I escaped any spanking, my mother was too happy to find Pavel.

One night our parents wanted to go to some Czech dance or so, and we were supposed to be left home. I did not like that, so I started to cry for them not to go. It didn't help, and they still marched out of the door. As soon as they were in front of the house, I came out on the balcony, and started to shout as loud as I could: "My parents are leaving me here without a dinner and hungry!" Boy, did I make a mistake! My mother came right back in, and the old wooden spoon had a feast, that I really felt hard, being only in my pajamas.

For us kids the life was great. Now, looking back I can imagine the stress our parents used to live under. Why is it, that only time and life experiences give us the right perspective on what is going on? How unfortunate that now, when we know all the answers, nobody comes to ask the questions.......

Then, as I said, finally came the end of the terrible war.

JUST ANOTHER ORDINARY LIFE

Clockwise from the top:
Aunt Jara, my parents, aunt Bozka, grandparents Marek, Pavel and myself, 1940.
Myself as 1 year old.
The factory grandpa Kolias, uncle Pepa and my father built, cca 1939.
Visiting mom's family in Germany, 1944.
Myself at Easter, 1940.

The end of war.

On the 9th of May 1945 the end of hostilities in war devastated Europe was declared. Happy and joyous people bearing flags, singing and dancing filled up streets. The six years of nightmare was gone! We kids joined wholeheartedly in the celebrations by running, screaming and jumping up and down. It was a great day, the full meaning of which we still did not understand fully.

The following days were full of fun, though. A whole group of us, neighborhood boys, would go to search and find unspent rifle and machine gun municions laying all around in sand by the river. We would find a large metal barrel, place it on a top of a low sand dune and build a fire in it. Then, laying behind another low sand dune, we would throw the bullets into the fire, hide immediately and wait for the munition to explode, bullets whistling over our heads. Luckily, our parents never found out about this adventure, or I am sure they would put an immediate stop to it. As it goes, kids seldom realize all the dangers involved in their "plays".

One of the first things to happen was the transformation of schools from the German curriculum to the national one, and I started to attend regular classes, too. My school was located on the other side of Kranj, and took me some 45 minutes of brisk walk to get there. At those times people were not concerned about kids walking alone being kidnapped or otherwise abused like today.

My mother had a different, unknown to me, plan for my education. Right after the war the whole country started to be run by the partisans with a strong Russian influenced Communist slant. It was obvious that one dictatorship was being exchanged for another. That, of course, did not set well with my freedom loving parents. It was decided that I will go to Czechoslovakia to be educated in a free and democratic society. We were all bilingual, so there was no problem with my fitting in the Czech classrooms.

As many other Czechs had a similar notion, a bus was dispatched from the Slovenia capital city Ljubljana via Austria to Czechoslovakia. So in June my Mother and I together with Aunt Boza (pregnant at that time with my cousin Vera) bordered the first bus, every seat filled, for Czechoslovakia. It was just a regular bus, no air conditioning, no bathrooms, no service.

Despite the hot summer days the mood on the bus was very festive. People would sing Czech national songs to tunes played on somebody's accordion, and the whole two days journey was quite pleasant to me. I remember that when we crossed the borders to Czechoslovakia, people there welcomed us very nicely, some even bringing fresh fruit and cold drinks to us. All that was very special, and lots of fellow bus passengers cried tears of happiness.

After arriving to Prague, my mother took me by train to a small village Masov situated on a hill overlooking larger town Turnov. My mother's Uncle Vojtech Marek lived there with his wife Hermina and three adult sons, Vojta, Evzen and Dusan, who all were already out of the house. Vojta worked as a goldsmith and sculptor in Prague,

Evzen was in the army and Dusan studied painting at Arts Academy in Prague, the Czechoslovakian capital.

So here I was, nine years old when my mother left me to be living with two, unknown to me, older people. Of course, my feelings were mixed. The house I now lived in was a very small one, consisting of an entry hallway in the middle of it, off which to the left was the kitchen and to the right the only bedroom. That was all. The house my uncle rented did not have electricity nor indoor plumbing. There was a hand operated water pump in the hallway connected to a well under the house. The toilet was an outhouse just across a narrow, unpaved way opposite to the main house entrance. As for the light we would use acetylene lamps and candles. My uncle worked at the Turnov rail station as a clerk and as such was entitled to some carbide that served as the source of acetylene gas for the lanterns. Lumps of carbide were placed at the bottom of a round metal cylinder capped with a small metal water storage tank, from which the water would drip down on the carbide, thus releasing the acetylene gas that was brought to the top of the lamp in narrow tube. There the gas would be lit by a match and produce a small, about an inch long, open flame just large enough for me to be able to read by it at night.

I did not have any toys there, so reading and helping with the house chores was my main occupation. My aunt Hermina wore thick eyeglasses, and still had difficulties to thread a needle, so it was I who would do that for her when she would mend our socks or attach lost buttons. She would go to clean houses for people, so her rough hands bore marks of her occupation. Uncle Vojtech was a teatotaller, and played quite decently his violin. Just about every night he would come to the bedroom (I slept with them in the same room) at my bedtime, and would play for me until I fell asleep.

Uncle Vojtech also rented a patch of ground nearby to the house where they would grow potatoes. Of course, I helped with tilling, seeding, watering and harvesting them. Another job I helped with was candle-making. I remember using thin square layers of wax where a wick, made of a piece of twine, was placed at one end of the layer which was subsequently rolled-up and formed a candle. There also was a small garden with some apple and pear trees in it. Adjacent to the outhouse there was a small wooden structure housing three rabbit bins. To feed them fresh grass from the garden was my duty. I liked to do that as I liked to touch rabbits and observe them eat. Oh, and when there were rabbit babies, I loved that the most.

In September I started to attend school. The school building was down an unpaved road from our house, about half a mile distant. I did know the language, but I did not know grammar which in Czech language is very difficult, some even say that it's one of the most difficult of all languages. Also, my pronunciation was slightly different which did not help when the other kids made fun of me. Let me tell you, being a new kid on the block, and a carrot red-head on top of it was not much fun. I was a constant target of all kinds of pranks and ridicules. I remember when going home from school, the kids would not let me use the road. I had to use a ditch on the side of the road, full of stinging nettles and other weeds instead. One time I got so mad at one of the biggest bullies, that I pulled out my pocket knife and threatened him with it. Strangely enough, that bought me some respect, so at the end I was able to make few friends there.

Being an avid reader helped me to advance at school rather quickly, so ever since reading is one of my best hobbies, and I find an old Czech saying that "a book is your best friend" very true.

Right after the war (remember, this is still 1945) there was a constant lack of food staples. To ensure that everybody would get at least some, food rationing coupons were issued to everybody by the government. For Christmas, as I was just a kid, I was issued a coupon for a chocolate bar! There was only one store in Turnov that carried them. So, one day, after school I embarked on about 4 miles long journey for the coveted bar of chocolate. Coming to the store I was surprised by about 100 feet long line of people all wanting the same thing as I did. When finally I got it, I started running back home to share the precious delicacy with my aunt and uncle. They took just a very small piece of it each, and until now, I can still feel the sweet goodness of that chocolate bar on my tongue as I gobbled it down.

The Christmas was fast approaching with cold weather and snow as it's forerunners. I was doing much better at school, and my Czech grammar was beginning to be almost perfect. For some reason throughout all of my school years, at all levels, I did not have difficulties learning any subject, and was always amongst the first three students in my class. As such I was awarded with a book of poems "Kytice" ("Buquet") by Erben, one of the Czech most admired poets, by my school. I do not remember what else I got for my first Christmas in my new country, but that book is forever embedded in my mind. Much later I learned that my mom, too, was very fond of the same book, and was able to recite long poems from it by heart even when she was over ninety years old. Ever since I remember a gift of some book was always there (and much anticipated) for Pavel and I at every Christmas or birthday.

My cousins would come home for Christmas, too. I remember one time, when the youngest, Dusan, was looking for something in my uncle's closet suddenly came up with a flat flask labeled as a brandy. It was about half full, and Dusan could not believe his eyes. "Now look at my dad, the non-drinker!" he exclaimed taking a healthy swig out of the bottle. "What the devil...." he shouted spitting the "liquor" out, making faces. Only later he learned that it was some anti-moth liquid to protect my uncle's woolen suit.

Winters are quite long in the central Europe, and the hilly Masov was no exception. At the upper end of the village, right where the forest started, was some fifteen feet tall natural granite tower Hlavatice. The members of the local tourist club chiseled steps into it, and placed a cable fence on the top, turning the stone in a much known look-out place with a commanding views over the city of Turnov and the valley it lays in. For us, kids it was a perfect starting point for downhill sled races that often ended in a crash into a heap of snow. Coming back to my uncle's house and its coal-burning stove induced warmth was a very much appreciated moment. My aunt would pour warm water into a large metal dish, placed it on a stool and I, standing in it naked, would take a sponge-bath trying not to splash water all over the wooden board floor.

A year passed by, and I was finally happy and settled down under my aunt and uncle excellent care, but it was time for me to move on, as my family circumstance changed once again.

Miroslav Kolias

Clockwise from the top:

With my father and Pavel just before departure for Czechoslovakia, 1945. With uncle Vojtech and aunt Hermina in Masov by Turnov, 1945. At aunt Bozka and Uncle Victor wedding in Liberec, 1947. With Babka Marek, Pavel and cousins Vlastik, Mirek and Jirka (aunt Jara and uncle Vlasta's boys) in Liberec, cca 1953. With Dusan and Vojta (Voitre) Marek in Masov, 1946. Dusan and Voitre became very famous painter and sculptor in Australia where they emmigrated with my mom's help in 1948-1949 via Germany, together with Evzen (Eugene). Darrin is Eugen's son.

To Liberec

In the meantime, in Yugoslavia the Communists under Tito were taking the government into their hands completely. Guided by the Soviet Union (Russia nowadays) and International Commintern (the Communist organization dedicated to expanding Communism all over the world) the nationalization of all privately held businesses started.

In this respect my family, for their good standing toward the new government caused by all the help given to Partisans during the war, was lucky. Our mill was supposed to get some kind of incorporation with the State and my family was offered to keep running it as managers.

Babka with aunts Bozka and Jara also returned back from Germany, and as there was nothing to come back to, they occupied the basement in our house. Grandfather Marek being dead, their economical survival in Yugoslavia was in peril. They all decided to return back to Czechoslovakia. My aunt Jara met a very nice, tall and handsome man, also from Kranj and of Czech origin, Vlasta Schneider in Munich during the war. He, too, was there as a forced laborer. They got married, packed all their meager belongings, and joined by Babka and aunt Bozka boarded a train and went to Liberec, large city in northern Bohemia to start a new life there.

The train was guarded by Partisans on its way through Yugoslavia and Austria. The trip took several days. My aunt Bozka befriended one of the guards, lanky and agile Croatian Viktor Drly. Croatian and Czech languages both belong to the Slavic group of languages so they could communicate pretty well. Viktor belonged to the Partisans from the beginning of the War, was awarded several medals for bravery and got the rank of Lieutenant. In Austria he decided to continue with the Mareks into Czechoslovakia, and settle down also in Liberec.

Liberec, situated under a 3,300 feet tall mountain Jested, in a very green, hilly valley used to be one of the principal towns of the so called Sudentenland. To understand all this, we have to dwell a little bit more into the history of Czechoslovakia.

After the World War One the Austro-Hungarian Empire, under the auspices of the U.S. was divided into several independent and democratic states. The similar region history and natural boundaries played a large role in forming these new states. The Czechoslovakia was formed on the 28. of October 1918 and consisted of Bohemia (with capital city Prague), Moravia, Slovakia and Ruthenia, totaling some eleven million people and situated right in the center of Europe. Its first President was a professor T. G. Masaryk, well known for his humanitarian ideals warmly embraced by the majority of the new state population. Bordering Bohemia on the west and south sides are three mountain ranges that served as its borders with Germany on the west, Austria on the south and Poland on the north. Easternmost Ruthenia bordered newly formed Soviet Union.

Especially on the west and north-west of the new state there existed a large German minority. This largely German region was called Sudety or Sudetenland in German language. As all the other national minorities (Hungarians, Poles, Austrians) they also enjoyed many privileges as in education, national recognition etc. When Hitler and Nazi Party in Germany in the mid-thirties got to power, the German minority largely sympathized with this German movement. The sympathies grew to outright rebellions and demands of the Sudetenland being recognized as part of Germany. The problem was that in those surrounding mountains Czechoslovakia built a great belt of defensive installments, one of the best in Europe, rivaling even the very well known, Maginote Line in France. This natural and man-made defensive line against German expansionism was taken away from Czechoslovakia by the infamous Munich Agreement that was designed to appease Hitler's appetite for "more land for Germans". As history proved, it did not work. Nazi Germany started to swallow Europe piece by piece during the World War Two.

After Germany was defeated, the German minority in Czechoslovakia was ordered to leave the country and go to Germany. Each person was entitled to only 55 lbs of belongings to take with them. Close to a three million people thus left Sudety, where a sudden and large people vacuum occurred. The Czechoslovak government started to ask all Czechs and Slovaks living abroad to return back home, fill this vacuum and help to start rebuilding the state consisting now only of Bohemia, Moravia and Slovakia. Ruthenia, that have had historic ties to Russia, was "awarded" to Soviet Union as a payment for helping to free Czechoslovakia from Nazi occupation.

In Liberec, too, many houses and factories were empty and waiting for people to come and occupy them. Therefore, the Mareks did not have any problem finding apartments to live in and jobs to sustain them.

Babka Marek with aunt Bozka got a nice apartment on a second floor of a large apartment house, aunt Jara and uncle Vlasta got one nearby, and so did Viktor Drly, who also, being a car mechanic by occupation, started to run a car repair shop.

After they settled down, my mom (still in Kranj) decided that I should go to live with Babka, as aunt Bozka and Viktor were going to get married.

And that's what happened. After my profound thanks to uncle Vojtech and aunt Hermina I left Masov for Rochlice (the part of Liberec where Babka lived) to start a new, so different from sleepy Masov, chapter in my life. Babka was very happy to have me with her, and she kept spoiling me to no end. Her apartment was right by the movie theatre. It did not take me long to befriend the proprietor whom I persuaded to let me help two other boys to clean the place after the first showing. As a reward we were let to see all the flicks we wanted. When the theatre was sold out (yes, it did happen) we were allowed to sit on the top of large central heating radiators. I do not have to mention that after such a seating our behinds felt like if they were freshly butchered. But we endured that and saw all the wonderful movies (some in color, no less!) like The four feathers, The thief from Baghdad, The Jungle Book and many others the names of which already escape me.

Since it was the time of school vacations, Babka enrolled me in the local Boy Scout unit, that I just loved. The Scout Master prohibited the other boys to make fun of my hair, and I made friends easily. One week-end our troop went for a two night stand into the not so distant woods. We packed the tents, sleeping bags, flashlights and other necessities and off we went pulling and pushing little four wheel wagon for some five miles to a little pond for our adventure. And believe me, for the ten-year olds, an adventure it was! The nine of us were divided into three tents, and every tent was responsible for the whole day meals for all, where eggs, potatoes, bread and Spam (a delicacy brought to us by UNRRA, postwar support to Europe from US)) being the main ingredients. We also had to keep watch at night, starting at ten, changing every three hours and ending at seven in the morning. My turn was from one after midnight to three and I still remember the clear sky, cold air and all the spooky sounds of "wilderness" that haunted me.

In Rochlice was also a large, open public swimming pool which I utilized as much as possible. Often, I would also visit Viktor's garage, and help him with some small errands. When aunt Bozka and Viktor decided to get married, I was part of that, too. The marriage ceremony was a simple one in the City Hall, aunt Bozka decked in her best outfit and Victor shining in his Partisan parade uniform with all the medals gleaming on his chest. So Babka and I were left alone in her apartment.

The two months of vacations went like water under a bridge, and I started to attend the fourth grade there. Every school day in the morning I would walk alone about a mile to school and back home again. On very few occasions my uncle Viktor would come to pick me up on his 500 cc BMW motorcycle to deliver me home, me just bursting with pride on the back seat.

Shortly after that my mom, dad and Pavel, together with uncle Pepa, aunt Boza and the Kolias grandparents also decided to come back and help to rebuild the country. I was very happy to be reunited with them after one and half year of absence. I had so much to show them, and especially to Pavel! Few very happy days followed. Suddenly both, Pavel and I fell very ill. The doctor's diagnosis was an ominous one: Diphtheria! Now remember this was before all the antibiotics, and the disease was considered life threatening.

Pavel and I ended up in Liberec Hospital infectious ward together with some ten other people in the same room. After the high fever subsided, we were still kept in the hospital for another five weeks for observations. One of older patients there had a chess board with him that I showed interest in. For nothing else to do there he started to show me how to play chess. I took an instant liking to the game, and this love is in me until today. Another diversion was to watch, from our second story window, games of handball on the adjacent school yard. I remember, when the ball ended up under our window, us shouting at anyone coming to pick the ball up: "Do not touch it, we have diphtheria and we spat on it!" causing a problem for the players. After few instances like this someone complained at the hospital office and the windows got nailed down shut. Oh, well..... I dedicated more of my time to learning chess, and started to show the game to Pavel, too.

Luckily, we did get out of the hospital with flying colors, and without any side effects. One boy however, about our age, sadly, died of diphtheria while we were hospitalized there.

In the meantime, my dad and uncle Pepa were traveling the country looking for some suitable abandoned factory to start a textile mill again. The political circumstances in the country started to get uncertain, though, so they decided not to pursue their dream and take an employment instead.

JUST ANOTHER ORDINARY LIFE

Clockwise from the top:
The "Castle" we lived in in As, 1947.
Pavel with Bella in As Na Haji, 1950.
In Dvur Kralove as an instructor, 1952.
In Dvur Kralove, 1952.
Our "Quartet" in Dvur Kralove, 1952.

The second beginning.

After aunt Bozka married uncle Viktor, they moved to Chrastava, a small town about 10 miles west of Liberec. Uncle Viktor took over a small scrap-metal business located on a property with a cute one-story brick house standing on the bank of a narrow river.

Since my family didn't have a permanent residence yet, Pavel and I moved to Chrastava with them. Aunt Bozka didn't have a regular job, she was just keeping papers for Viktor's business, and both of them welcomed us there warmly. For Pavel and I, both fresh from the hospital, this move brought us free days that we spent mostly in the small river bathing and trying to catch some fish or crayfish. We didn't have any fishing rods, so we invented a unique way to succeed.

We would get apart some 10 feet or so, close to one of the banks, stick our hands under the water and started to move slowly toward each other, at the same time trying to feel in the bank crevices for fish. Surprisingly, we did catch some! Not many, though, as the fish were very slick and quick to get away from our searching hands. I do remember aunt Bozka making a meal from our catches about two or three times for us.

Uncle Viktor had an old U.S. army Chevrolet truck for his business. He was very proud of the "old clunker" as we called it, and treated it with lots of TLC. Sure enough, it served him well, and I always had to chuckle when he in Czech would say "Chevrolet na sto let", which translates " A Chevrolet is good for hundred years". This was our first exposure to American car industry. We liked it a lot.

After couple of months, I believe it was by the end of 1946, my father landed a job in the country westernmost town ss (pronounced "ash"), right on the border with West Germany. He became a head of three large textile dye houses located in As and nearby village Krasny Potok (Beautiful Creek). The latter one was the largest of the three. It came with a very large, three-story house built of stones in some kind of medieval architecture with an adjacent tower, looking like a real old castle. The original mill owners, the Jagers, were still living there, but in the process of moving out, just like the rest of Germans from Sudetenland.

As the head of the company my father was let to have this "castle" to live in. All the furnishings stayed in after the Jagers moved out, so we could move in right away. Uncle Viktor loaded Pavel and I in the "old clunker" and started a whole day some 200 miles long journey from Chrastava to Krasny Potok. After getting there late at night, we could not believe our eyes.

We will be living in a castle!

The huge entry hall, serving also as the main living and entertainment room, boasted a beautiful, six feet wide, polished wood stairway into the second story. On the first landing an enormous, framed hunting scene painting covered the whole wall. From there the stairway continued onto the second floor. Besides a large stone fireplace in the main hallway, there were also side rooms, one furnished as a hunter's room with preserved heads of elks, bison and wild bores overlooking a full standing black bear. It was said that Mr. Jager himself shot all the animals on his hunting trips around Europe. The other side room was appointed as a lady's sitting room with a marvelous pink alabaster 4 feet tall statue of Greek goddess Diana. For us, kids, it was just like living in a fairy tale.

Finishing the first floor was also a large dining room and similarly large kitchen with a walk-in refrigerator. The coal burning stove was fed from an adjacent hallway, so there would be no coal dust in the kitchen. Pavel and I each got separate bedrooms on the second floor. It was the first and also the last time we would have separate rooms. The largest bedroom was occupied by our father and mother.

The grounds around the "castle" (we all referred to our living place as such) were also impressive. Besides a tennis court, there was a large vegetable garden, and some 30 acres of meadows, three large ponds (one even with its own island) and a fenced range for wild animals. Fruit bearing and flowering trees and shrubs were scattered all over.

Pavel and I started to go to school in Krasny Potok right away. We had to go along the largest pond, through the mill's entrance, down the road, and up a long hill, all together some 2 miles or so to reach our school, which was a small one, just two classrooms large. The first and second grades were in one, and the third, fourth and fifth grades were in the other classroom. Our teachers were very strict with us, quite understandable under the circumstances. We would be sitting by two, straight up with our hands tucked behind our backs, taking them out only when writing or signaling for an answer to teacher's question. Each grade section would be working simultaneously with just one teacher teaching us all. Much later, after reading stories about how the west was won here, in the U.S., I would visualize those schools like the one in Krasny Potok. Again, I was bullied by my fellow students for my red hair. One time I got again so mad that I tore off a fence plank and broke it over the back of the biggest bully. It worked again, and I was left alone. From then on I got smarter, and every time I got into a new school, or was introduced to a new friend, I asked everybody to just call me Rusty. This did the trick. Everybody knew me as Rusty, and there was no more bullying.

We've lived in the "castle" for almost two years, spending our time playing in the fields, bathing in all those ponds or using our leather school bags as sleds going down the hill in winter. Once I even fell through the first and still thin ice into the very cold water on one of the ponds. Luckily it was just by the shore, so even though wet, I could get out rather easily.

At the end of 1947 and the beginning of 1948, the political climate in Czechoslovakia started to get a new turn. The Soviet Union mingling prevented the Czechoslovak government to accept the very favorable and great Marshall Plan offered to all the war ravaged countries in Europe by the U.S. The elections of 1946, showed large gains by the Communist Party, buoyed by the fact that the Soviet Army liberated the vast part of Czechoslovakia. Despite that the Communists ended only the second strongest, the winner being the Social Democrats, also left oriented, while the National Democrats, the right oriented party were a strong third.

Now once again (sorry about that) is time for another history lesson.

After the first President Tomas G. Masaryk, a son of a farm worker, died (by the way, the G. in his name stands for Garrigue, the name of American lady Miss Alice Garrigue that Masaryk married while studying in the U.S.), his close collaborator Eduard Benes was elected President in 1938. While Masaryk was nicknamed "The Liberator", Benes' nickname was "The Builder". As far as I can tell, Benes was a great humanitarian, but he was rather a meek person, but still well loved by the population. After the humiliating betrayal of the Munich dictate, when Benes was not even allowed to sit on the negotiations between France, England and Germany concerning the Sudetenland, Benes practically lost the Republic to the future Hitler's expansionism. In March 1939 the whole of Czechoslovakia was occupied by German troops. Benes, together with the whole government fled the country into England, where they formed a pro-western government in exile. Similarly, in 1940 after Germany attacked Soviet Union, despite their non-aggression treaty, a pro-Moscow oriented Czechoslovak government led by Gottwald was formed in Moscow. Both shadow governments were trying to influence the thinking of the Czechoslovak population by radio broadcasts and various help in the fight against Nazi occupiers. When the U.S. allied itself with Soviet Union and Great Britain in the fight against Germany, the German troops started to lose the war in Europe. The final division of Europe after the war was discussed and agreed on in Yalta conference between F. D. Roosevelt, Winston Churchill, De Gaulle and Josef Stalin. Unfortunately, already ailing F.D.R. did not heed bulldog Churchill's advice, and gave in to foxy sly Stalin persuasions to create the so-called Demarcation Line dividing Europe from North to South, which later on became the infamous Iron Curtain. Czechoslovakia fell, unfortunately, into the Soviet (Russian) sphere of interest. That's why when U.S. armed forces at the beginning of May 1945 liberated Pilsen (yes, the same town the Pilsen Beer comes from), it had to stop there and wait for several days until the Soviet army reached Prague from the east. On the 5th of May the Peoples Uprising of Prague occurred. People dismantled centuries old street pavings to form barricades from it to prevent German tanks to drive through. They were hoping that by involving German troops in fights in Prague streets, the Allied forces would easily reach Prague from Pilsen within a day. Unfortunately, the Yalta agreement prevented that, and the population of Prague was decimated by German army. On the 8th of May finally the Soviet troops reached Prague and declared themselves the liberators of all Czechoslovakia. On the 9th of May the war in Europe ended.

This was the political situation right after the war. The legitimate president Benes' government came home from exile and so did the Moscow "government", backed by the strong argument of Soviet liberation of the country. A political tug-of-war started from which a new government emerged headed by Gottwald. Another key position the Moscow faction got was the Interior and Defense Ministries. The rest of positions were filled by people from the original, pre-war government that came from London. Uncertain times for Czechoslovakia ensued. Pressure from Moscow grew steadily stronger, culminating in the February 28th 1948 Communist putch, in which the head of the Social Democrats, Mr. Fierlinger simply, and possibly unlawfully, declared all its election votes from the last election to become in fact votes for the Communist Party. The pro-western Ministers came to President Benes and offered an abdication. The idea was that he would reject that, forcing new elections. Benes, facing the results of Yalta Conference, received their abdication and later on abdicated under duress himself also.

The full-fledged Communist rule started after that. Gottwald was elected the President. All the industry and banking were nationalized, the previous owners were partially imprisoned, partially placed as regular workers, in now the state owned factories, some even tried and shot or hanged. Their families became blacklisted as "class enemies", meaning the enemies of the working class which was the preferred segment of population. Once classified as the class enemy, all the advancement at work, higher education or a position in any leading capacity was not possible. Each person had a dossier in the City Halls and in the Police Departments into which everything was being marked, from the names of friends one would have, if one attended church, what party affiliation one has, if one participates in various Communist celebrations etc, etc. All press and broadcasting were strongly censored, the international broadcasting in Czech language was affected by whirring sound to become impossible to hear, the travel abroad was mostly for a good standing Communists, even the inner travel in the country was monitored. In every apartment house, for example, was one individual whose duty was to register anyone staying overnight and report to local authorities. Every citizen was issued a Citizen's Identification book that had to be carried on a person all the time. This book contained your photograph, your address, your place of work, your date of birth and the police could stop any individual at any time to produce this document without any good reason.

The whole country, just getting from the German occupation and enjoying the newly acquired freedoms was suddenly and brutally thrown back into the dark ages. People who wanted to avoid being caught in this mess, tried to escape across the border into Germany. My mom, always being the rebel, living right next to the border grabbed this opportunity to show her disdain for the new regime by organizing a network of people who would help her friends to cross the borders. Suddenly we would have strangers coming to the "castle", and staying overnight, or even for few days. Amongst others, I remember, was a prominent tennis and hockey player who was kind enough to let me play ball with him on the tennis court. At some other time, my cousin Dusan from Turnov would show up and later on Vojta and Evzen did the same. Still another was a couple of young people from Prague, Mr. and Mrs. T. who wanted to cross the border, but were detained by the police. While on the police station, being interrogated, Mr. T., who used to own a dyeing and cleaning establishment in Prague (now nationalized), remembered my father being the head of dye houses in As. Mr. T. declared that they just lost their way, and ended up close to the border by mistake, as they were unfamiliar with the country there. They were just trying to find their way to my father, who promised to give them employment in one of the dye houses.

Of course, no such promise was made. My father had known Mr. T. just very little from the time he and uncle Pepa were considering opening a dye house for themselves. The police called my father to his office and asked him, if he knew Mr. T. to verify his statement. My father in some strange moment of clairvoyancy said that yes, he does know Mr. T., and is expecting his visit. Based on my father's word the police released the couple. My father by his quick thinking saved them from a long and harsh imprisonment. Mr. and Mrs. T. stayed with us for few days until my mom arranged their safe crossing into Germany.

Under the Communist regime.

My mother was also vocal about the unfairness of the Communist putch. According to the new Constitution, anyone who would try to undermine the new regime was committing an illegal act of treason. Together with the "unusual" activities around our family, my Mother was in 1949 detained by police, and subsequently and quickly sentenced to nine months in local jail.

Since my father would have to go to work, Babka had to come over from Liberec to take care of Pavel, my father and myself. I remember being able to visit my mother in jail in the whole time only once. When my mother got home from jail, she was employed as a sales lady in a sporting goods store. I liked to go and help her as much as I could and at the same time get familiar with all the new sport equipment.

As a warning to my family, my father was demoted from running the whole complex of mills, to head just one of them. Only his excellent knowledge of the dye business saved him from being demoted into some manual job. Also, at that time the "castle" was converted into the home for Greek children. In Greece at that time a civil war was raging between the Communist and pro-western factions. Consequently, lots of children lost their families. Some of the children from the Communist sympathizers were thus brought into Czechoslovakia to be cared for there. One of the places they were housed in was the "castle" which was perfect for such an enterprise.

Our family was moved into a nice three-story unfurnished apartment house sitting in a large garden just overlooking the factory my father was now working in. We were on the top floor, the only occupants there. The other two apartments were empty. Pavel and I shared a large bedroom with doors leading into the hallway and another one on a balcony overlooking part of the garden. There was another bedroom, a large living room, a hall, a bathroom and a kitchen with doors leading to yet another just a small balcony overlooking the other (western) side of the house.

Just at that time we got a nice German-shepherd female dog Bella who had her dog house on that small balcony. Bella was a smart, large dog we boys had a lot of fun with running around the house and garden with her.

Since our new apartment was part of the city now, Pavel and I had to go to new schools. By then I was already attending so called Burgher School (Mestanska Skola). The school system in Czechoslovakia was as follows: At six one started a five years Grammar School. After that one had to make a decision of going either into a four-year Burgher School or eight year Gymnasium. The Burgher School was a general education school, geared for either being the end of schooling, or preparing students to continue at some technical education. The Gymnasium, beside the general education, was geared to prepare students for University, more humanitarian education. Since my whole family were technicians, it was preordained for Pavel and I that we, too, would follow in their footsteps.

I forgot to mention that I was a member of the Boy Scouts in As, too, until the whole organization was closed down by the government as a "reactionary" movement sometimes around the end of 1948. The only children organization allowed was the Pioneers, modeled after it's Soviet counterpart. This did not sit well with me. The whole situation in the country was very difficult for kids of school age. In school only the Communist doctrine was taught, tinting everything, especially the history. Suddenly the Soviet Union was the only shining example of everything. For example, the western-born inventors would always be mentioned only in passing, while the Russians were the ones who made all the technical innovations. I remember a widely circulated joke about this situation:

"Do you know who invented the telephone? No. Ivan Popov, of course. He stuck one end of a wire in his ear and the other one in his ass and heard shit!"

Our and other parents, of course, would try to correct this situation by teaching us the real things, causing uncertainties in the young children's minds. There was also a constant danger of kids at school opposing this new, state ordered views, exposing thus their parents to reprisals by the regime. Demotion at one's job or even a jail time would be a frequent punishment. It so happened, that I and another boy, Karel (also a former Boy Scout), got on a warpath against Communists. When staying one day overnight with Karel, we sneaked out of his apartment in the middle of night, and went into the sleeping town. Karel had addresses of people who were actively involved in the new regime. We would seek their houses and throw stones through their windows. Well, when we were at the sixth address, we were caught and taken to the police station.

Well, what could they do with twelve years old kids? We were interrogated (I was told that for sure one day I will end up hanging from the gallows!) and finally taken to our respective homes. Since Karel was living with only his mom, and they had to struggle to survive, I took the whole caper on myself. My parents had to pay for all the broken windows, I got good spanking from my father, and as an additional punishment I could not attend a school trip to Moravia's famous caves Macocha, that I was really looking forward to. Karel, too, was similarly punished.

To make up for that we started to wander around a lot. There was so much to discover everywhere! Most of small, once vibrant and producing mills were now empty, their machinery and equipment standing idly, partially due to lack of manpower after the Germans were sent off to Germany. The doors to them were either open, or one could get in simply by climbing through broken windows. I remember finding a room full of already molding fashionable lady's straw hats adorned with artificial flowers and ribbons. In another mill we would discover "secret" narrow underground passages, full of metal pipes, leading to unknown destinations. We just had to crawl through them, flashlights in hands, ending up in a large boiler room. Someplace else we came across various chemicals in large metal drums, glass containers and cardboard boxes, all fallen down on the floor, strewn around. Of course, we had to try to mix them together, marveling over colorful, fog-like fumes they produced. It really is a miracle that we did not end up dead or at least severely burned. I only shudder now, imagining that my own child or grandchild would be doing something similar.

I remember one day running with Pavel across a large empty meadow (most of farms around were still empty for the same reason as above) when we came across a small, shallow pond. It was a hot, sunny day so Pavel and I welcomed the chance of getting into the water to cool down. "Ouch!" Pavel would suddenly exclaim. Reaching into the water he started pulling out a whole chain of machine gun bullets! Another one soon followed. And another! "There's got to be a whole stack of ammunition in there" I said. Suddenly our dangerous plays with munition back in Slovenia came to my mind. I visualized retrieving soldiers, throwing their, not any more needed burdens into this pond. "Let's drain the pond to find out!" A small dike was holding the water behind it. It didn't take us too long to find an overgrown draining box with a rusty gate in it. It took all of our combine strength to pry the gate loose and pull it out. After a while the water was gone, leaving muddy bottom in its place. Wading through the mud we pulled out a small ammunition arsenal, including some hand grenades. Some of these were the round metal ones. Returning home and bringing hand held canvas bags back was the next thing to do. Filling the bags about half full, so we could handle them, and finishing them with freshly cut grass (in case a policeman would stop us and inquire, we would tell him that it's grass for our rabbits) we moved all the munition in a deep wooded ravine near of our house. In the next few days, we would dig holes in the side of ravine and hide our treasure in, covering it with bush branches and grass. Many days afterwards we would come secretly to this place and would throw the hand grenades into a marked circle few yards away, laying quickly down after each toss, just in case they would actually explode. Well, one day coming for our "exercise" we spotted a bunch of policemen there clearing the whole thing up. I don't know, how they found out, but, luckily, Pavel and I were never interrogated about it.

One day, after coming from work my mother started a serious conversation at the dinner table with us. "I know that the Secret Police is watching us" she said. "It might not take long, and they could be at our throats again". She said that she arranged for us to cross the border into Germany. We were to come to a certain spot in woods after 10 PM, and somebody would guide us across. So, we packed a small suitcase for the four of us, and after the night fell embarked on a voyage that should end in a free world. Before we left our apartment, my mom wanted to break all our furniture with an ax.

This was the furniture my parents bought with small part of money they received as payment by the Yugoslav Government for their part of the mill in Kranj. Unfortunately, the money was paid directly to the Czechoslovak Government which, in turn, put it into a so called "restricted account". The same was true for uncle Pepa's and grandfather Kolias' parts. Both, uncle Pepa and my father applied for the money, but were allowed only a very small portion of it, which was just enough to furnish our new apartment. Uncle Pepa, together with my grandfather bought a nice house in Novy Bor for themselves. The bulk of the money was never forwarded to us, practically, it was stolen by the Czechoslovak Government.

Anyway, my father always being of non-controversial nature talked my mom from destroying the furniture. After getting to the spot and waiting there with trembling hearts for about an hour, the supposed guide came and told us that the whole thing has to be cancelled, as there is some unusual patrol alertness along the borders, so crossing would be very dangerous, especially with children involved. So it happened that we had to return back into our apartment, luckily with the furniture intact. This, and many other times, my father was right in that that one should not take extreme actions without thoroughly understanding the consequences. I got the message laude and clear!

To be fair, though, not everything was bad under the Communist regime. Schools at all levels were free, medical care was free, everybody was entitled to a job, everybody was entitled to a place to live in, and everybody was entitled to minimum of food staples. There were no homeless people wandering the streets. Of course, all this has to be also viewed from a little bit different angle. All the above was granted to anybody who followed the Communist rules. Who did not, their kids could not get any higher education. Towns were divided into sections and anybody living there had to go to the doctor who was in charge of this particular section. If he was not a good doctor, well, too bad! Everybody got a job, but everybody also had to work. Who, for any reason, would not want to work was considered as "parasite of society", promptly put in jail and got a forced, unpaid job. The food staples, at least for a few years, a family could get by bringing food rationing coupons to a grocer. Since there was a constant shortage of everything, one had to stand in a line (sometimes for hours) to get them. Perhaps the capital, Prague, was some exemption because foreigners would visit there, but the rest of the country was poorly off. Since apartment houses were owned by the state, they were not repaired properly, housing was poor. To alleviate that the state started to build thousands of multilevel sparsely equipped concrete panel apartment houses. These apartment houses were built very quickly, without proper street paving, so when it rained (and that is often there) their occupants had to go out in rubber boots to avoid getting all muddy. In factories the pay for a certain job was virtually the same for anyone anywhere, since under the Communist doctrine everybody was equal to another. That is with the exemption of the Communist hierarchy, who had their privileged, well stocked stores to shop in and enjoyed all kinds of other special perks. Since the pay was practically the same if you performed well or not, most of the time people did not put too much effort in whatever they were doing. The sales personnel at stores were annoyed when you wanted some help from them. The economy thus started to get down the drain rather quickly.

In short, if one towed the line, he could "enjoy" a meager living, without worry of job or health coverage, but was deprived of so many other things, like free communications, trips abroad, free mind and speech, free movement within the country, free choice of what to read or listen to, etc., etc.

The apprenticeship years.

In the summer of 1950, at the age of 14 I started to go to work in the dye house. I only worked for few hours a day, just to get familiar with what my future occupation is going to be. As a third-generation textile dyer, I was eager to learn everything and was looking forward to go and attend a special school to properly learn my trade.

Before that I have planned another memorable event in my life. It was the last year of basic schooling, so the four of us, Jarda, Herbert, Edy and I decided to go for a two week back-packing trip to southern Bohemia. Yes, we did! I don't remember how I persuaded my mom to let me go, but one fine June afternoon we were all at the train station buying tickets to the part of Bohemia we never visited before.

The southern Bohemia is the land of fairy tales and strange happenings for centuries. It is also very beautiful, sunny, full of streams, lakes, hills and deep forests, sprinkled with medieval castles and baroque mansions. We had hardly any money. All meals we had to cook ourselves. Edy was supposed to bring a cookbook along, but it turned out to be a vegetarian one. Well, actually it was

OK, because our diet consisted of half ripen fruit, potatoes we dug on the sly from potato fields, green peas, stolen cucumbers and such. We would sleep under a tent, skinny dipping in early morning fog in a river or a pond. Marching through lovely countryside we would sing old tramp songs and tell jokes. We visited some castles, some mansions and a friend of Herbert's. Generally, we were tired, hungry, dirty, sunburned and cold, but immensely happy. A trip like this happens only once in a lifetime and it cannot be forgotten. Many years later I even wrote a thin book about it called "The ship diary" just for my enjoyment. Well, frankly, we were also glad to be back home again without any harm coming to us.

At the end of July, I got my first long pants (until now Pavel and I would only wear short pants with cotton stockings in wintertime), got a huge suitcase my mom packed for me, and embarked on a day-long train journey to Dvur Kralove in north-eastern Bohemia. Coincidentally, it was the same town my father at one time attended College and my Grand-father ran a textile printing division of a large textile mill in the early 1900's. Later on, when visiting the Textile Museum there I was fortunate to find an old book full of textile prints that was dedicated by my Grand-father by writing: "Started with God's help" and a date (which I already have forgotten) and my Grand-father's signature.

After changing train two times and lugging my suitcase along, I arrived to Dvur Kralove and boarded a bus that took me and other co-passengers from the train station to the town main square. After asking for directions, I arrived to the boarding house belonging to the Trade Textile Profession School, my next home for two years.

This and many other similar schools were dispersed throughout the country, their goal being to teach kids who finished the basic schooling some profession or trade. Depending on the difficulty of any given profession, these schools would last a year, two or three years. For example, my school offered the following courses:

One year courses:

    1/ Yarn Spinning and Cloth Weaving

    2/ Bleaching

    3/ Final Textile Finishing

Two year course: 4/ Fabric and Yarn Dyeing

Three year course: 5/ Engraving and Fabric Printing.

When one would finish any of these courses, he or she became a professional capable of handling any job offered in his field. Besides all the technical courses, math, physics, chemistry, history and Czech language were also taught.

My boarding house consisted of a whole third story floor of a large and old factory warehouse building refurbished to accommodate about 80 students. There was a central hallway running the length of the floor with rooms for six students on each side of it. Each room consisted of a narrow fore-room where simple metal cabinets (without locks) were placed, one for each occupant and the main room with six metal single beds, each with a night stand, and a small table with two chairs. Two large sectional windows overlooked the street below and two central heating radiators prevented us from freezing in winter time. A loudspeaker, operated from the dorm governor's room, in one of the corners completed the room furnishings. It was rumored, that through this loudspeaker the governor could also listen to our conversations, but I am not sure of it. As it happened, in my room there was also a locked door to an unused elevator shaft. This extra feature proved to be very useful to us later on. After being able to unlock the door, we would use the shaft as a storage for forbidden, into Czech language translated western cowboy story magazines some of us had at home from the "good old days".

At the beginning of the central hallway there was a small room used as an "office" for an attendant selected from one of us, students, changing daily. His duties (this was an all boys establishment, the girls were housed in a different building nearby) were to take our mail to the post office, bring incoming mail to us, arrange visits with a doctor and generally keep an eye on the whole floor. On the opposite side of the hallway was a large bathroom with several wash-basins, showers and toilets. Hot water was available only twice a week for showering. At the end of the hallway was a room occupied by the dorm governor responsible for a smooth running of daily affairs. At one side of his room was a large recreational room with a ping-pong table, serving also as a projection room for occasional movies which, for our endless delight, were attended also by the fellow girl students. On the other side was another large room equipped with tables and chairs. There we had to quietly spend two hours daily studying after school or writing letters home after that.

The life in such a boarding school was a very structured one. At six o'clock the loudspeaker woke us up with some progressive march. A run into the bathroom followed. After washing up in cold water, each of us would have to make his bed and tidy up the whole room. At seven we would gather down on the street and marched in a column (sometimes singing) to a nearby school cafeteria for a good and nutritious breakfast. After that was another march through two streets and across a river bridge either into the school or in the factory. On Mondays, Wednesdays and Fridays we had to go to school while on Tuesdays, Thursdays and Saturdays we would go to the factory for practical learning. The factory was a complete, up-to-date equipped textile mill where we would, under the supervision of very good professionals, do all the work required to finish regular job orders. I guess that whatever money these completed jobs brought in were used to partially finance the whole establishment, as the students did not have to pay anything. At noon we would go to lunch, and at three o'clock back to our dormitories. After washing up and studying it was time to go to dinner. On Sundays we got a permission to go to a movie (again as a group) and on

JUST ANOTHER ORDINARY LIFE

Wednesday after school we could go for an hour to the town to buy some necessities. Smoking was strictly forbidden. Whoever would be caught smoking, his hair was shaved off. Alcohol or drugs were not a problem at all. Of course, throughout everything there always was a Communist propaganda twist present. The central mottos: "An individual means nothing, the common good means everything" and "Who is not with us is against us" were curtains behind which the total dominance of one's life was conducted.

To get a little bit more free time for myself, I started to do various sports. First, I learned how to play ping-pong, and was able to get to represent the school in some tournaments. The best place I achieved was the fifth overall. Handball was another sport I enjoyed. Two other boys from my room, Zdenek and Jirka were also on the same team. We were actually doing pretty good, competing against about ten other teams from the neighboring towns in our category. We placed second overall, which gave us some small privileges in otherwise so tight boarding school life.

All my life I liked to sing. Zdenek and Jirka had good voices, too and another member of my room, Tibor, was quite an accomplished guitar player. Together we formed a group and managed to entertain local parties and gatherings, free of charge, of course.our awards were good food, lots of fun and time away. Our repertoire consisted of popular songs and we even tried some humorous skits here and there. All this we would start by ourselves, without any official help or prodding. We were just kids wanting to express ourselves in any good way possible since we felt that our lives are too constricted. By looking at all this now, I think that a well structured and strict life is very beneficial to young people of this age. Even though we didn't like it many times, the advantage of it is obvious. I remember our governor, when we would complain to him about the strictness of our school regime, he would reply: "As long as you complain about this, I know that I am doing my job right!"

Interestingly enough, despite all of these side activities, my grades at school and at work were always amongst the best of my class. That, too, cut me some slack occasionally.

The calendar year was coming to an end, and we who were from a very distant locations could, finally, also get home for some time off. The local people could visit their families twice a month for over the week-end. We did not have access to a telephone, so we had to keep in touch just by an occasional letter or receiving a parcel with goodies that I shared with all my room cohabitants. I was looking forward to see mom, dad and Pavel after long time. I went to the town and bought for each of them some small presents. As a kid, I never had much money on myself. Even here at the boarding school we were completely taken care of, our laundry was made, we were well fed. All we needed was some pocket money, supplied by our parents, for an occasional movie, lemonade or candy. We did not have girl-friends yet, so any extra money I spent was when out of town for a ping-pong or handball match and that wasn't much.

So I packed my small suitcase, boarded bus for the train station, bought my one-way ticket to As, and settled down waiting for the train to arrive.

The dark day.

I heard the playful whistling of the steam engine pulling my train into the station, and was happy to get on it. The train was only about half full, so I selected a seat by the window and enjoyed the ride overlooking fast moving scenery outside. The railroad went by banks of briskly flowing river that had to jump over thousands of boulders on its way down the canyon. White water was everywhere. What a sight! Sudden darkness of tunnels, carved into the stony canyon sides, interrupted this beautiful view occasionally, adding depth to the exhilarating experience.

After an over an hour ride, I had to change trains in Pardubice, large town with sprawled train station accommodating many intersecting railroads into all directions. I was a part of many hundreds of passengers milling around, finding their ways to different trains when suddenly I heard: "Mirek, Mirek!"

Turning around I spotted my uncle Pepa trying to reach me. "What are you doing here?" he asked. "Why, I am going home for my vacations" was my reply. "What do you mean home? Don't you know anything?" "What should I know?" "Well, I don't know how to tell you this, but your folks are in prison" was uncle Pepa's incredulous answer.

The sky fell down onto me.

Uncle Pepa took me aside, and in the middle of all the hubbub explained what happened.

"I don't know all the details, all I know that the Secret Police came and took both your parents into prison. I cannot believe that nobody would let you know that."

So did I. Only much later I learned what really happened. My mom was working with a group of other people on a scheme how to get us all out of the country. There was this train that originated in Cheb and ended in As. The railroad from As across the borders to Germany was not, for some reason, obstructed. Normally the train would turn around in As and go back to Cheb. The group of people working on this caper wanted to assemble their supporters in such a way, that they would operate the steam engine, and also be train conductors all at the same time. The scheduling had to be done very carefully, without suspicion. This group was supposed to take the train across the border. As it happened, one of the regular, not conspiring group turned ill unexpectedly, and had to be replaced by one of the conspirators, putting them together early than planned. Since it happened at the last moment, my parents, who were supposed to be also on that train with us kids, could not get the word to me in time to be in As for the train's departure. They were forced to stay behind. The so called Freedom Train got across to Germany as planned. All the co-conspirators were on it together with their families and friends, as well as a lot of regular passengers. Actually, some of those took the opportunity and stayed in Germany, too. Others came back after few days, together with the train. When the word got out about the train departure, my mom ran into the street and was showing her pleasure about the news. That was enough for the Secret Service, who was watching my parents anyway, to get them both imprisoned. When Pavel, eleven at that time, got home from school, he found our apartment sealed. By the door there was a bag with some of his clothes left for him outside. That was it. No message, no nothing. Pavel, not knowing what to make of it, waited until dark, and when nobody showed up, he went to the neighbor's house asking if they would know what has happened. They were very kind to him, fed him dinner and let him sleep at their place. In the morning they were able to get the police to open our apartment and Pavel was allowed to get our dog Bella out. Nobody knew aunt Bozka's (the only one with a telephone) phone number. After the good neighbors gave him money, Pavel was able to get to the station with Bella, buy the necessary tickets and take the train trip to Liberec to Babka. It took him three changes of train and the whole day to get there. How he accomplished that all by himself is still beyond my comprehension. Babka, too, did not know anything. She was able through aunt Bozka to send a word to uncle Pepa in Novy Bor. He didn't think that I wouldn't have known what happened, so he did not try to get in touch with me. All this was happening in the last two or three days.

Uncle Pepa was on his way to see some customers, and he, too, had to change train in Pardubice. That's how it happened that he ran into me there. It surely seems as some mysterious good hand was extended over me, and prevented me to go to As.

After thanking uncle Pepa, I went to the train station office and told them that I changed my mind about going to As. They cancelled the rest of my ticket and issued me a new one back to Dvur Kralove. What a different ride from the morning one this was! I was constantly on the verge of tears. What was going to happen to Pavel and I?

Aunt Bozka and uncle Victor did not have any children, while aunt Jara in Liberec had three, younger than us boys, cousins Mirek, Vlasta and Jirka. Aunt Bozka was happy to take Pavel in, and she practically raised him up, bless her heart! I was in the middle of my first year in the boarding school, so that, too, was OK. From now on, for my vacations I would go to Liberec to Babka and aunt Jara.

    I did not tell anybody at school what has happened to me. When I was asked why did I return from my trip, I faked illness as being the reason. I do not know for sure if the school staff knew about my plight, but I do suspect that they did. In any case I acted as if nothing happened, and continued in all my activities and schooling as before.

Coping.

The rest of the two years schooling was a pretty difficult one for me. I had to follow the official political course otherwise I would have been expelled, and keep good marks at school, since I did not have practically a home any more. The latter part was not a problem. Again, I was at the top of my class.

Keeping up with the rest was not so easy. I hated the regime that broke up my family, but had to appear to be towing the line. For a young, impressionable boy this is not a simple task. I learned to keep my thoughts for myself. Fortunately, the whole situation did not affect my ability to keep friends, participate in all programs at the boarding school, and continue with our little singing "quartet" as well as with my sport activities.

One day Uncle Pepa asked me to come and go with him to my Father's sentencing. My Father was not really involved in my Mother's activities as they understood the perils that could come to our family. One of them should be available to Pavel and I in case my Mother's activities would be compromised. That did not stop the authorities to charge my Father as my Mother's accomplice, though, but on much lesser scale. He was accused for not reporting my Mother to the authorities!

Under some pretense I got permission to leave school for the trip with Uncle Pepa to Karlovy Vary, the County seat to which As belonged. After we arrived there, we were able to see my Father at the Courthouse, and even hug him. I noticed that his ill-fitting, prisoner pants were held in place by a thick, dirty rope. I took off my leather belt and gave it to my Father in exchange for his rope which I then kept for many years. My Father was sentenced to a year of heavy labor. He was given a choice of working either in a sulphuric acid producing factory or in an uranium mine in Jachymov. He chose the uranium mine, where he subsequently worked for the whole year. We never could visit him there.

Later on, after his release he would tell us about the very poor working conditions in the mine and in the labor camp. He would work with murderers and other political prisoners like himself. He would be working stacking up some 50 lbs crates of pure uranium ore eight of them on the top of each other. He called that "orgies of work" as the crates would be arriving constantly for the whole ten hour shift. Totally exhausted he would come back to the camp for some poor food and was able to get some rest in a room with about twenty other prisoners.

Sometimes, he said, he would be directed to go and clean underground mine tunnels from various debris. There would be water constantly dripping on his helmet with a little battery light attached to it. On one of such days he started a conversation with some other inmate, who would tell him about his family leaving Bohemia just before the World War 1, and settling in Argentina. After very difficult beginnings there, in time they would get some land free of charge from the Argentinian government. The only condition for keeping the land was to clear trees from it and to build a well and an outhouse, all within a year. After that the land became theirs. Eventually they built a prosperous ranch on this land, raising cattle and pigs. After 1948 Communist takeover of Czechoslovakia he would subscribe to Rude Pravo (Red Justice), the Communist daily from Prague. In it he would read about the good life people now have, about the equality of everybody, about the fact that everything was nationalized, and thus owned by all of the people. He would fall for this propaganda, took his entire family and came back to Czechoslovakia. His friends tried to persuade him not to go, but to no avail. So they, at least told him that they will keep his ranch there for him, and in case things would not go as planned, he could return back. Anyway, when they all arrived to Prague, their passports were confiscated and he and his wife were assigned a job in a factory for wages that were incomparably smaller than what they earned in Argentina. They were also assigned a small flat to live in. His two kids did not know Czech very well, and had a lot of troubles in school. His wife hated the constricted and very structured life there, too. So after a while he decided to send the wife and kids to Germany to "visit a friend". After long time he was able to achieve that, but he could not go with them himself. That was a common government practice, so people would always have to come back to rejoin their families. One adult or the kids would always have to stay behind, practically as hostages. After his wife and kids left, he tried to escape across the border to Germany to join them there, but was caught in the process and consequently sentenced to 15 years of hard labor.

No family member was allowed to get to my Mother's trial. The process was in front of a secret State Court in Prague, and the prosecution was asking for a death sentence! The reason for that was that my Mother has helped some 235 people to cross the border to Germany. The problem was that she never took any monetary compensations for her services. The prosecution alleged that she did it because she despised the regime and thus committed a treason. If she would have been paid for her services, she would have been regarded only as a greedy person, and sentence would have been much more lenient. At the end of the trial my Mother was given 22 years in prison, though. Out of that she would serve 10 years. Later on she never wanted to talk about her time in prison.

During her imprisonment she would be moved from prison to prison, and work at various places. Twice a year I and/or my Father, who was released from his one year sentence by then, would be allowed to see her. I remember one occasion where she would be working out in the fields gathering potatoes, that we would be able to actually come to see her there, and would be able to even leave some food for her. When we would visit her in actual prison, we would be lead around heavy machine-guns and into a room, where we would be able to spent 30 minutes with her. Those were very hard times for us, kids.

I remember another visit, when she was working in a kitchen of some farm. My Father and I came to see her, and were able to actually sit down with her for several hours. She gave me a small, about 2" x 2" square, hand made booklet. It was made of cardboard paper clad in printed fabric, and decorated all around with golden yarn stitches. In it my Mom wrote: "To Mirek from Mom" on one side and the other side she wrote a quote from a well known poet Jan Neruda: "If each of us will be hard as stone, the whole nation will be of a rock". It was very symbolic to me, and I carried it in my wallet for many, many years even brought it with us here, to California.

The first year of my schooling went by. I got accustomed to the situation and kept coming to Liberec for my days off. Babka, Aunt Jara and Uncle Vlasta became my adoptive family. Babka especially was very good to me. She would see to it that I would always have some money on me. She gave me 500 Koruna bill (quite a bit of money at that time) which I never spent. Instead, I would carry it in my wallet in a side, semi-secret compartment. It became a habit for me, and I always try to have some extra money hidden on me.

The second year started and with it a group of new students would come in. We, now the "seniors", would be moved to a smaller, cozier building. Our "quartet" managed to keep in one room together. The rooms, too, were smaller, just for the four of us and we really enjoyed our life there. In about a middle of the second year, after consulting with my Father, I decided to ask and try to get to the 4 year Textile College in town as good students from my school were given preferential placement there. I knew that it would not be a problem for me to excel there. When I approached my school master with the suggestion, he just looked at me and curtly said: "That's out of the question for you!" I knew exactly why that was. I was classified as an enemy of the Communist establishment because of my parents and as such was not allowed to attend any regular higher education school.

"Well, so be it" I thought and just kept working toward my final exams. At just about that time I met a girl, Masha, who was in school to become a textile bleacher, her studies lasted only one year. Any little free time we would have we tried to spent together, and, naturally, fell in love. Relationship like this was frowned upon by our school masters, so we had to keep it secret.

The two days of final exams came and I passed them with flying colors at the head of my class. As a reward I was put into one step higher classification group then my schoolmates. Those classification groups were rather important. When we would get a job, each group was paid a certain wages, regardless if one would be working here or someplace else. As long as he or she would be working at a certain position, this position was paid very similar wages. There might be some small differences based on the length one would work at a certain job, but otherwise the pay was the same. So being awarded a higher classification group, it was significant (and based on my "status" surprising) to me. On top of it I was asked to stay in the school factory as an Instructor of the dye house for the incoming group of future textile dyers.

I gladly accepted that, since my Father, after being released from prison, did not have a place suitable for me to live in with him. He was working as a laborer in a small dye house in a Northern Bohemian town Mikulasovice. Before I was to start my new Instructor job, I was given a week of paid vacation. Masha, too, finished her schooling and was supposed to return home to Moravia. We decided that we would spend a week together, under a tent, tramping in Central Bohemia on the river Sazava that was always regarded as a Mecca for all outdoor loving young people.

And so we did.

Later I have learned that when Masha got home much later than she should have, as soon as she walked into the room her father smacked her across her face. The distance kept us apart, and gradually we both found different ways in our lives.

After graduating.

I loved the Instructor's job. I had a good group of just a little bit younger people then myself, and established a very good working relationship with them. After work, though, it was different. Our "quartet" did not exist any more, my friends each went back to their hometowns scattered all across Bohemia, and we lost touch. As an Instructor I was assigned a room for myself in yet another building, where I would have to pay rent and also pay for my meals. The wages I was earning barely were enough to sustain me. Quite often, when the chance came, I would volunteer to work extra time, usually at night from 10 till 6 in the morning, on top of my regular day duties. The money was fine, but lack of sleep and exhaustion took its toll on me.

When visiting Babka in Liberec, she didn't like what she saw.

My Father, in the meantime, became (because he was a first rate dyer, despite his unfavorable political classification) a Dyehouse Manager in a large textile company MILAX headquartered in Ceska Kamenice. My Father moved to Ceska Kamenice and took my brother Pavel with him there. Pavel was just finishing his basic schooling, and wanted to learn to be a knitter of textile goods. Since MILAX had a knitting factory in Ceska Kamenice, Pavel started a job there living in my Father's apartment. They grew pretty close during that time. My Father knew a dyehouse manager in Liberec, and asked, if there would be a place for me to work at. As it happened this dye house just installed a new continuous cloth dyeing machine. Since it was very expensive piece of machinery, some 80 feet long consisting of multiple vats with various dye and rinsing baths in them, they were looking for experienced people to run it. We at school did have a similar, older type machine and I was very familiar with it.

My Father would call me and ask if I'd like to work there. It was a great opportunity, since I would be able to live with Babka and have a good, better paying job. It didn't take me long to accept.

The only trouble was that Babka lived in one part of Liberec, while the dye house was clear on the other side of the city. Not many people owned a car at that time, except for Uncle Victor nobody in my family did. Luckily an old street car connected different parts of Liberec. One station was about a mile from Babka's house, and after changing trains at midtown the other one would bring me to the front of my workplace.

The job was an interesting one. New machinery, new processes, new people to work with. In short time we were able to have it running beautifully. I met an old friend Honza there, who was also with me at the textile dyeing school in Dvur Kralove. That was a nice surprise. We became quite good friends. Honza owned a motorcycle - a two stroke 250 ccm Czech manufactured JAWA two-seater.

Honza invited me to spent a week with his family in Southern Bohemia in part called Sumava, famous for its woods, fog and hills. His parents welcomed me warmly and Honza proudly was introducing me to his boyhood country. We even went dancing to a village nearby. Well, we were seventeen already! On his JAWA we would travel all around and really enjoyed ourselves for a whole week.

Working in Liberec was fun. Babka would take a good care of me and since she lived in an apartment, there was not too much for me to do after work. Honza and I and some other similarly old friends would go to the town, have a coffee and a very good dessert in one of the small bakeries, go swimming in the public open swimming pool, wander in the woods of nearby mountain Jested or took a cable car on it's very top, some 3,500' up and enjoyed the sweeping views of Liberec and it's surroundings.

I also joined the factory sport club Jiskra (The Spark) where I would in wintertime represent it in cross-country skiing, and in summer time I was a part of youth soccer team. I kept myself busy as much as I could.

Toward the end of fall my Father asked me if I'd like to go to Krasna Lipa, where the largest MILAX's dye house was situated. An opening for a shift dyer happened there, and I was offered the position. It would mean my moving to Krasna Lipa, find a place to live in and generally take care of myself. Quite a challenge for a young man like myself, being in charge of a whole shift consisting of some twenty five mostly seasoned workers. After just short trepidations I accepted!

Krasna Lipa is a small town of some 3,000 inhabitants at the very north part of Bohemia, close to (at that time) East German and Polish borders, part of the now practically people empty Sudetenland. From Liberec it takes a little over an hour of train ride through mostly abandoned fields and pastures, beautiful wooded mountain sides and along several streams. I liked it. After getting to Krasna Lipa I learned about the town's history. It was a very well known textile town specializing in producing lady nylons and cotton, woolen and half-woolen fabrics and yarns. Dyeing all these different textiles was just what I was trained to do. The company

I'd be working for consisted of two buildings situated on the two opposite sides of the town. The first branch was a cotton and half-wool knitting factory producing both, lightweight and heavyveight fabrics. The second branch (the one I'd be employed at) would dye fabrics, dry, calender (machine ironing) and package them. Both branches were running at three 8 hour shifts. I was, as a newcomer, assigned to the night 10 PM to 6 AM shift and was to start the very same day.

That left me with just few hours to try and find a place to live in.... Fortunately someone suggested that a friend of his is having a large house with even larger garden who might be willing to sub-rent a room for me. The house was situated about a mile walk from the factory, and the lady of the house who opened the door to me, after checking me out thoroughly agreed to rent a room on the first floor to me. As a bonus the rent also included hot breakfast.

Great!!! The first floor of the house held three large rooms (the largest being some 450 (!) square feet), tiled hallway, toilet (with only a commode and cold water wash basin in it) and passageway out into the garden. There also was a bathroom with a bathtub and a large copper coal burning water heater. That was a part of my landlord's apartment on the second floor to which some 4 feet wide, stone staircase with a landing in the middle was leading. It was a grand, about 70 years old house with large coal cellar and a room with a brick oven holding 3 feet wide brass kettle servicing as a laundry room. My room was about 9 x 12 feet with a 10 feet high ceiling and two double windows sitting in 24 inches thick wall. A wooden, double winged 7 feet high door lead to it from the hallway. There was an electric portable heater, a small table with two simple chairs, a wardrobe and a bed there. It was pretty cold, and it was not winter yet! The room became my home for the next about a year. I remember that in winter time, after coming home from work around 7 AM I would find a tray with now cold coffee and two pieces of butter-and-jelly bread sitting in front of my door, and inside the room water in my free standing metal wash bowl frozen solid. I wouldn't heat the room, wolf down my cold breakfast and went to bed in some 15 F degree room.

What a difference from Babka's gentle care!

After waking up around noon or so, I'd wash myself in the cold water and go to the factory for lunch, provided there for all employees for a very minimal price. After lunch I'd usually go back to my room, turn on my heater and either took a nap or did some reading, mostly technical stuff as I discovered that I do not know everything I needed to run a shift. Around four or so I'd go to town to meet friends, that I gradually got, to play table-tennis in local club or went to the gym to play basketball and voleyball there. Before getting back to work I'd get something to eat, like a sandwich or so. For the week-ends I'd go to Liberec to Babka's or to Novy Bor to Uncle Pepa's, where I'd also meet with my Father and Pavel who would come regularly from Ceska Kamenice. Uncle Pepa's house was a large three story high villa sitting in a very nice, quite large garden. Besides Uncle Pepa's family consisting of Aunt Boza and cousins Vera and Honza, Grandpa and Grandma Kolias, Aunt Ella with cousins Otta and Ernst and Uncle and Aunt Neumann (Aunt Boza parents) also lived there. Being all together, we always have had a good time there.

In about a month I joined the local amateur theatre club. It was headed, fortunately, by a man with vast theatre and vaudeville experience. We would put up funny skits, some serious plays, too, and travel with them into surrounding towns as well as performing in front of our town audience. Since I started to work at 10 PM, I had enough time to learn my roles, and soon became one of the leading members of the troupe. I guess the saying "Amongst the blind the one-eyed is the king" was well suited for me. I loved it, though!

Living in a small town, where everybody knew everybody was, I guess, good for us, young people there. Of course, we would get into some mischief occasionally, but in general we were behaving because we were under a constant supervision of the town folks. People did not have much moneis available to scatter around, everybody was making just enough to sustain himself and his family. When a Doctor's or Firefighter's after Christmas dances would be in town, that was a BIG thing. Everybody went! The young ones would sit around their tables, the older ones around theirs. We had to (more or less) behave well, so we would not get a bad report into our "Profile" kept in everybody's employment place. There would be a person assigned to keep these "profiles" up to date. Your behavior, work ethics, if you attended a mass (that was not recommended), if you attended Communist rallies (highly recommended), in short everything and anything you did was scrutinized and judged. One had to be careful not to get in trouble. Especially someone like myself who was not looked upon (from the official standpoint) very keenly. To keep my position at work I had to tow the line again, especially when my Father was back in the supervisory and decision making role.

In few months one of the day shift dyers was assigned to a different position and I was offered his job. I welcomed it, since I developed some stomach troubles, probably from lack and irregularity of sleep. Running a day shift was quite different than running a night one. At night I was there all by myself making decisions and controlling working procedures. On the day shift I became a part of the whole production, not only the dyeing part. I was also much more in contact with other production brass and under their watchful eyes. I think that I pulled my weight well, though.

The spring and summer went by and in the fall of 1955 a was drafted to a two year duty in Armed Forces! Every man of Czechoslovakia had to go for two years to the service. Only those who would be found physically or mentally incapable of service were excused. Students in the process of studying got an extension, and would have to go after they finished their studies.

I knew about the law, but somehow forgot about it. The actual draft order caught me by a surprise. I only had a couple of weeks to get all my things in order and report to Liberec for the unpleasant duty. Before that I had to go to Novy Bor to appear before the Draft Commission that was supposed to deem me fit to go and defend my country against the "American imperialists". To satisfy that a whole bunch of us, draftees, had to completely disrobe, form a single file line and one by one stand in front of four medical doctors who would make a short, but thorough examination of our barely developed bodies.

Well, I passed with flying colors, together with everybody else. After that was time to celebrate. We all went to a local bar and started to drink beer with a shot of rum in every glass. The result was predictable. After so many of them we were all intoxicated, barely standing on our feet, screaming nonsenses at each other.

It started to rain. I do not remember how I got to Uncle Pepa's house, but remember Aunt Ella waking me, completely soaked through, up on the front lawn and taking me in. My Army duty was starting!

Miroslav Kolias

Clockwise from the top:

With Honza (the JAWA motorcycle) in Liberec, 1954.
As a shift dyer in Krasna Lipa with Ing. Beyer, spring 1955.
I rented the room with the first window from the left in our future home in Krasna Lipa, winter 1954/55.
As a soldier in Opava, spring 1956.
As a soldier-miner in Ostrava, spring 1957.

In the Army.

It was in the fall of 1955 (I do not remember the exact date anymore) when I reported to Liberec Army barracks that sported a large banner over the main gate: "WELCOME, DRAFTEES" - it said. Jokeingly we would say that on the other side of that banner, not visible to us, was also written: "WE'VE GOT YOU NOW!"

Well, my two years of soldiering did not start badly. We, some three hundred strong, were treated to a very good lunch served by pretty civilian girls, on real china placed on tablecloth covered tables. Little did we know that this was the last real china and tablecloth meal we would have for the next two years.

Next in order was disrobing and receiving our uniforms, underwear, sleep-wear and black high boots called for some reason half-liters. Our civilian clothes were packed in a bag and stored until we would be discharged. The final step was getting rid of our hair. Long line of "barbers" we're ready to cut our precious curls, so meticulously groomed before.

Almost bald-headed and in ill-fitting uniforms we had to march to local train station to board a train to our still unknown destinations. Only after we were safely on the way out of Liberec I was told that my destination is Opava in Northern Moravia. A whole night journey ensued, and in the morning, sleepy and tired we arrived to Opava which turned out to be a very nice city with a long history as a capital of Silesia, Moravian region on the Polish borders.

There was about a hundred of us, marching in an overclouded early morning through the town to the large 19th Century barracks housing a big guns brigade. Four large three story high buildings formed a rectangle with paved, sprawled plaza between them, our future home.

"New ears are here!" shouted the resident soldiers when we marched in through the large wrought iron gates. They were happy since now they will be the old ones there, the ones who will be able to make life miserable for us, newcomers, just like a year ago, when they came in, the old soldiers were making life miserable for them. Yes, history does repeat itself!

Our boot camp was on the third floor of the largest building facing the main gates. We were housed fourty to a room with twenty iron bunk beds, two night stands by each of them, and a large coal burning stove in the corner of the room. I selected a bottom bed which, I found later, was not very smart, as fine straw dust kept falling on my face whenever the guy over me turned at night. Our mattresses were filled with straw to a hard, unyielding cube whose loosely woven covers allowed the fine dust to seep out from them.

The boot camp lasted for six very hard weeks. By six in the morning we were all awakened by blaring music from two loudspeakers in the corners of our "dorm". At the same time the door would burst open by couple of unfriendly looking sergeants shouting at the top of their voices: "Let's go!!! Let's go!!!" after which we had to jump out of our beds, and clad only in our long night shirts had to run into a large wash-room with a row of urinals on one side of the wall, and a row of metal throughs with cold water spigots in them on the other side of the same wall. On the opposite side of the room was a row of open front toilets and open shower stalls. Hot water was available only twice a week.

After a quick cold wash, we had to run back to our rooms, quickly put on our pants and boots and make our beds up. That was not a simple matter! Each bed had to be covered by two heavy blankets completely wrinkle free, in a form of perfect rectangle with sharp edges on each side. The pillow, fluffed-up and smoothed had to be placed exactly in the middle of the bed. All that was done under constant shouts and yellings of our commanding sergeants. A mad run of half naked "ears", prompted by more shouts, from the third floor down followed. Our heavy boots, sported large metal pin heads covering their soles, kept skidding on the tiled floors and steps resulting in many falls and tumbles down the steps. On each landing another shouting sergeant stood, laughing and enjoying our misery. Once out on the plaza we had to form groups and proceed with calisthenics for some twenty minutes, rain or shine. The original cold and shivers of our bodies gradually warmed up by it. After that another mad run, this time up the stairs, brought us back into our rooms. To our horror most of our beds were completely messed-up as they did not pass the sergeant's inspection and we, of course under another salvos of shouts, had to remake them quickly, then finish our dressing and run down again. After forming groups by each room, we were marched to the mess-hall for breakfast. Standing in a very long line each of us was issued two aluminum bowls with handles, an aluminum mug and a spoon. Those bowls, stretched out one in each hand would be filled with whatever was for breakfast that day by unfriendly scowling cooks. Large open drum of black, unsweetened coffee stood at the end of the food line so we could dip our mugs in and get some. Much later we learned that that coffee, consumed for the whole two years by us, was spiked by some special drug that was supposed to cut down on our libido.

Amazingly, all that was done very quickly and efficiently, without much problems. After eating at long tables and sitting on benches, we had to wash our utensils in a lukewarm water, go out, form groups, march and later run up back to our rooms, where a list of cleaning shifts were already posted. Whoever had a cleaning duty, got a metal pail, a mop, some rags and started to clean the some hundred feet long corridor, the bathrooms, showers and our rooms. "What is wet, is clean" was the motto which we all followed. Everything had to be done in some 15 minutes after which we had to run down again and started our regular training. For hours, in groups, we would "Turn left!, Turn right!, Turn front to back!, March forward!, Stop!" like automats which we all were actually supposed to be turned into.

Lunch and dinner processes were similar to the breakfast one, with the only difference being that after lunch we had to go back to our rooms and take 45 minutes "rest". That meant disrobe, put the night shirts on, mess up our beds, lay down for 30 minutes, get up, make the beds, dress up and run down to more mind dumming training. Sometimes, after training we would be asked questions like: "Who knows how to type?" or something like that. Usually, whoever lifted his hand up, was taken aside and later told: "Tomorrow morning at 4 o'clock you will go to the kitchen to peel potatoes!" or something similar. After this happening to me I quickly learned, while in the Army not to volunteer for anything.

After dinner that was at 7 o'clock we would go to a lecture room and were subjected to an hour of propaganda about how great the Communist system was, how terrible is life under the Capitalist establishments and how we have to be diligent in defending our system against the American Imperialists. Funny thing was that observing my fellow soldiers, just about everybody kept staring straight ahead, to the ceiling or to the desk not paying any attention to the "Political Lieutenant" talking his head off in front of us.

From 8 to 9 in the evening we would have an hour for ourselves. We could go to the lecture room, write letters, read or just talk in low voices. After that we could change into our angel-like night shirts and go to bed, of course clean and polish our boots and folding our uniforms up first. By 10 o'clock the light would go off (except for small emergency lights scattered around) and we would go to sleep. Sometimes our sleep would be disrupted by an alarm and we would have to get dressed and form our groups down on the exercise plaza. This would be timed, and if we did not do it in predetermined time, we could expect to do it again the following night. Yes, the boot camp is full of fun. Especially when after getting in our beds, a sergeant would come in and start to inspect how we folded our uniforms. They had to be folded into squares and placed on the night stands. The pants first, coat on top of them, underwear and shirt followed. On the top of the pile, that had to be exactly square from the bottom all the way up with matching edges, our cap would be put in the middle, and on it our coiled belt with the coiled tie inside it. The boots would be placed in front of the night stand. If the sergeant would not like what he saw, he would open a window and throw our clothes and boots out. Now imagine a bunch of guys, dressed in their long night shirts running three flights down and trying to find their belongings in the darkness of the exercise plaza down there! Well, it was quite common occurrence, in which, unfortunately, I often participated.

Each and every one of us hated the boot camp, and were looking forward to its end. I remember one day when I was assigned to cleaning the main stairway. I was in the middle of making the steps wet when a Major came in. I had to drop the wet rug, stand up, salute and tell him my rank, my name and my assignment. He looked me over and said:

"At ease, comrade soldier! For how long have you been here already?"

"For a week, comrade Major" was my shouted reply.

"See, don't you love how fast your two years are going by?"

Now, wouldn't you like to wring his neck? I sure wanted to! Yes, we were all "comrades" in the People's Army and had to address each other like that. Of course, that's where all the "comradeship" ended. Just like in any other army, everything went by the rank. That's why I was looking forward to the end of the boot camp. I was sure that I will be selected into the Underofficer School based on my civilian occupation. The school lasted six months (if I remember correctly), and after passing it we would get one or two narrow red stripes on our epaulettes, the sign of our rank.

To my astonishment I was not selected into that school. I wasn't given any explanation, but it became clear to me. Because of my Mom's and Dad's imprisonment I was not the right "material" for being in charge of anything here. Instead, I was assigned to a Surveyor Company. Boy, that was great! I did not realize my luck right from the start, but later on I really appreciated it. Our main function was to survey targets on the big gun training field in the mountains, selected for target-shoot practicing. Our Company would go there first and have to survey some 100 or so different targets, like an abandoned house, an edge of a forest, a clump of trees or bushes etc. I happened to be pretty good and quick with math, having a long experience in calculating dye formulas, so this was not a problem for me at all. Since we would be there all by ourselves, headed only by a second year, and actually friendly sergeant, we would have a great time. No hurry, no strict regiment, just a slow work surveying and marking surveyed targets in a Book of Targets and their numerical positions. We would be living in tents, cook for ourselves and generally having a good time.

When we would be finished with that, we would return in about a week, ten days back to our barracks, being usually assigned to work in the kitchen. That meant plenty of good food and minimum of debilitating practice how to march, turn and clean our rifles. Of course, we had to learn how to shoot a rifle and a pistol and everything a soldier is supposed to know, but we didn't have to repeat and repeat all that over and over again like other soldiers assigned to the big gun units.

The best times we would have at the actual target practices. There were four gun units in our Brigade, competing amongst each other in live ammunition target practice bombardment. Whichever Unit won, everybody was promised a free time to go home for a week. In turn everybody wanted us, who had to measure their bombarding efforts, to give them the best results. We would have food ready at all times we appeared at any of the four Units. Everybody was nice to us, everybody made friends with us, the Lord Surveyors.

Of course, that at the end of exercises every Unit fulfilled its assignments!

The whole Regiment got very good marks. All the Officers were happy and gained ranks!

Hooray for Surveyors!!

And so the first year of my "service to people" went on pretty good, I could not complain. Occasional passes into Opava me and my friend surveyors would spend in several dancing halls trying to get a girl at least to talk and dance with. In very rare occasions we would be able to do that. Most of the time they would just make a face and say: "I don't dance with soldiers!" Well, that was that! Even when rejected, we would still love to go out into the town. As much so that we would sometimes sneak out without a pass. Most of the time nothing happened, but once I was caught by the MP patrol and put in the brig for two days. It wasn't bad, I just had to clean officer's offices.

Sometimes I'd be assigned to a sentry to our Division Headquarters in town. Right behind the HQ buildings was a factory producing very tasty chocolate covered Fidor waffles. We would be diligently marching up and down the building back yard, making sure that nobody tried to attack it. We would serve four hour shifts out, four hours up in the sentry room, and four hours to be allowed to sleep. While out, marching between the HQ and the Fidor buildings, sometimes a factory window would open and a friendly girl working the grave-yard shift, would toss a Fidor waffle to us. If we would be very lucky, we could even set a next day date with her. Of course the HQ sentry was very popular and sought after duty.

Unfortunately, as the saying goes, anything good has to end someday. Based on some international agreements, our Army was supposed to lower the amount of its establishments. To do so our Brigade was put into mothballs and we, soldiers were shipped into different Army establishments all over Czechoslovakia.

I was assigned to Vyskov, one of the largest Army camps consisting of an elite big gun Brigade and the Officer School. A bunch of us came in from cushy positions and fell head first into the strictest regiment imaginable. Since I was still only a lowest rank soldier, I got all the "best" assignments like scrub floors of the Officer's Club or their offices. Now the floors there were made of wooden, unfinished boards that had to be scrubbed white clean. No "what is wet is clean" applied here. I was daily on my knees wielding the scrubbing brushes and trying to get rid of all the boot marks, dust and years old grime. I remember one instant when a Lieutenant came to check on my work. He did not like it. He got down on his knees, took the brush, and for some five minutes rubbed it in about a square foot of boards. They were white! "This is how I want the whole office look like" he declared and left me there, very unhappy. It took me a whole week to copy his square foot of floor!

I don't remember getting a single pass into Vyskov, a smaller than Opava town north of the largest Moravian city Brno. It was dreadful!

Fortunately, about two weeks later a special Committee with even more special assignment was sent to our camp.

JUST ANOTHER ORDINARY LIFE

In Northern Moravia, by Ostrava, are large and deep coal mines. For some reason there was not enough workers in them. So the Brass decided, since there was this unexpected influx of new soldiers, that they could spare some of us, and send us to those mines. We were all gathered in a large hall in front of the Committee. Now I am not a strong or stocky man, but I decided that anything must be better than what I was experiencing right now.

So when the question: "Who would like to go to work in the mines?" was put in front of us, my hand shot up amongst the first ones despite the reluctance to volunteer to anything in the Army.

And that was that. In a couple of days, I was called into the office and was given marching orders to Karvinna, north of Ostrava, very close to the Polish borders. About twenty of us boarded the train and in few hours long journey arrived to Karvinna station. Two Officers greeted us there and promptly transported to a four-story high, gray building called Eight hundred. Actually, I never learned the reason for its name. Perhaps there was eight hundred of us there? Who knows?!

The main thing was that we all became the "Blackies". These "Black" units got their name from the black epaulettes soldiers wore on their shoulders and were formed mostly of people who were not trusted to carry a gun. I, too, happily had to put my rifle in a storage room and became a "Blackie".

Miroslav Kolias

Clockwise from the top:

As the head dyer in Krasna Lipa with my crew, spring 1958.
Marta with my father on the New Year party, 1957
Herta with Rudi and Eva by their cottage in Opava.
Herta at her cottage.

A coal mining soldier.

Wow! What a difference! The whole special Brigade was practically outside the regular Army regulations. That meant no drills, no shooting ranges, no nothing! We would all be working in several deep coal mines in the famous Ostrava Coal Fields. These fields contained the best quality of coal anywhere in the world, called Anthracid. Formed millions of years ago by fallen trees and prehistoric vegetation, covered with rows of volcanic and tectonic material, deprived of oxygen, all this organic material slowly decomposed and under tremendous pressure of the overlaying dirt and dust formed vast Anthracit coal fields.

Generally, there are four types of coal. The poorest one would be the youngest, and resembles some kind of hardened, caked mud. This type of coal is not found in Czechoslovakia. Better quality would be the Brown Coal mined generally in very large open pits, scarring the pretty face of our land. Those fields were in Czechoslovakia mostly found in the North-Western Bohemia around the town of Most. A good quality Cole is the Black Cole, largely used in chemical industries, burning in electricity producing plants and gasification. Those mines would be around town Kladno, near Prague. As I mentioned previously, the best coal, the Anthracit, very black, crystalline and light-weight coal that actually sparkled under shining light, was mined right here, around Ostrava and Karvinna. That's why Ostrava was also full of large steel producing mills (all nationalized of course, just as all of the other industry was) making it a very important industrial center of Czechoslovakia, and actually of all of the so called "Eastern Block" countries under the direct influence of oviet Union.

Ostrava was not a pretty town. Many and many steel mills' black smoke belching high stacks created almost permanent haze over the entire region, through which the ever-trying sun only occasionally was able to peer down. Comparably the region was a wealthy one, because wages in coal mines and steel mills were the highest. Unfortunately, the hard and dangerous work was also very exhausting, so people were not keen on using their hard earned moneis for traveling and recreation. They tended to gather after work in very many local pubs and drink heavily. Hard work and poor eating and drinking habits took their toll on the wellbeing of locals. Lung diseases, caused by constant exposure to cold dust and soot, were prevalent. Cough, asthma, black lungs disease was very common. To suppress the unhealthy influence of this environment on children, children were often sent out of the region for a prolonged stay in the state run clean air spas throughout the rest of the country, mainly in the mountains. Still, it did not help much. The whole Ostrava environment was in very poor shape ecologically.

Since there was constant lack of workers, especially in the very deep (around 2,500 feet deep), coal mines, the "Blackies" were commanded to help. We would be housed in rooms of four "soldiers", were fed good food, and most importantly, were paid somewhat for our work. A regular soldier would be given a little pocket money each month, just enough to buy a movie ticket, get a beer or take a girlfriend out occasionally for a hot dog or so. The

"Blackies" on the other hand were comparably well off. We would all be earning a minimum wage, but since we didn't have to pay for room and board, it amounted to quite a bit.

All this we, the newcomers, learned in a week-long course as well as all the safety regulations of deep mining, the means and ways of coal mining in general and, of course, the way of conducting ourselves in public. Well, we were told what to do and not to do, but very rarely were actually checked on while out on the town, which was often. No more sneaking over the fence - after getting "home" from work, we were practically left alone to do whatever we pleased. Only about once a week we would be called into a large room and were given a speal lasting about an hour of how a soldier in the People's Socialist Army should behave and conduct himself.

Well, yes, we could endure that......

After finishing my Introductory course, I with many others, was ordered to go for an exploratory trip down to the mine called The Mine Of The May First. The given name was in celebration of May 1st, one of the most important Communist holidays, the Work Holiday. I have to confess that, after donning a black work garb consisting of pants, shirt and jacket and getting a helmet and hand-held heavy electrical lantern, my heart was trembling while marching to the elevator shaft leading way down under.

A large, poorly lit, three stories tall, lift cabin hanging on an arm-size cable was waiting for us on the top of the seemingly bottomless pit. After piling in, the cage's see-through door made of steel bars was shut close and we suddenly lost the floor under our feet! At least that's how it felt to us, when the cabin started plunging rapidly, almost soundlessly down. The cabin was "flying" down past several "floors" of the mine with waiting miners on each of them (we could see them as a split second blur hollering to us), and finally after several minutes (unfortunately I do not remember how many any more) we landed on the very bottom. The landing was not a smooth stop. Rather, since the cable was over 3,000 feet long and somewhat elastic, it consisted of several up-and-down movements before standing still. My stomach felt queasy, but here we were!

Almost suddenly a din of moving steel carts, compressed air powered metal picks, hissing of escaping compressed air, hollers and wind blowing surrounded us.

Wind blowing???

Yes, of course! Two thousand eight hundred feet below surface is a pretty hot and airless place. All the air for our breathing has to be delivered down there by system of ducts and huge ventilators blowing air down on one side of the mine field, and being sucked up on the other side of the field creating a constant wind.

We boarded a waiting compressed air powered engine pulled train, made of small covered metal cars, that transported us for couple of miles through about ten feet tall and twelve feet wide, fairly well-lit and by heavy metal braces braced tunnel to the end of the field. Throughout our rather slow journey we were able to observe the inner workings of the mine.

The whole field was several square miles large. In the middle of it there was the main shaft leading deep down. The field consisted of several variously thick layers of black coal (the upper layers) and Anthracit coal (the bottom layers) stacked on top of each other and divided by variously thick layers of dirt and stone. Something like a many layer chocolate cake. Two main tunnels, dug in a coal layer and equipped with narrow gauge double railroad tracks, ran perpendicularly from the main shaft to the opposite sides of the field, dividing the whole cake in two halves. Along the main tunnel there were large side rooms serving as various shops, shelters, rest rooms and such. After about every 300 feet another, smaller, secondary little up-sloped tunnels ran perpendicularly on both sides to the main tunnel into the coal layer, dividing thus the whole field into long, rather narrow, somewhat even sections.

Alongside the whole length of these secondary tunnels a wide conveyor belt ran toward the main shaft, ending over the tracks in a loading dock. The secondary tunnels, in just about every 600 feet, were now interconnected by yet another, smaller tunnels (running again in the same direction as the main tunnel) following the coal vein, finally dividing thus the whole field into sections of roughly 300 x 600 feet. That's where the miners actually worked on the 300 feet long coal vein wall, extracting coal, loading it on a narrower conveyor belt and making their way toward the main tunnel. The dug-out coal was transported by the narrow conveyor belt, spilled onto the secondary tunnel conveyor belt down to the loading dock under which open steel carts would be pushed one by one by the compressed air engine and loaded up with coal. After the whole train of cars was loaded up, it would be pushed to the main shaft and transported in batches of three cars up to the surface for further work. And so it went, on and on all two shifts long.

    The miners in those side tunnels were positioned between the conveyor belt and the coal layer, called "the wall". Now imagine the conditions we had to work under. It's hot down there, around 90 F, water, seeping from above, constantly dripping all around from the overhead "ceiling", fine coal dust everywhere, din of machinery, hissing of escaping compressed air and poor light. Talking is impossible, shouting being the only way of communication. Now, if you are working in a tall layer, standing up, you can consider yourself lucky. Unfortunately, deep down here, there are layers of coal much thinner than that, some only as thin as 3 - 4 feet! Well, surprise, surprise, those were the ones reserved for us, soldiers! The goal of deep coal mining is to get out only the coal and leave the top and bottom layers of dirt and rock as much as possible intact. Practically, of course, this is not 100% possible, that's why the whole excavation had to be sorted out on the surface. I was never involved in that kind of operations.

Miroslav Kolias

The first mining job I got was relatively an easy one. I was working the first shift, from 6 AM till 2 PM.

The actual coal digging shifts were always the 6-2 and 2-10 PM, while the cleaning and preparation for the next day shift lasted from 10 PM till 6 AM. Well, those were the hours we would clock in and out on the top of the mine, before and after we would go down and up to or from our actual work place. The transportation down and to the work place took over an hour, sometimes (to the very far sections) even two hours. After we would all arrive, the foreman would give us our daily assignments. That took another about 15 - 20 minutes. So, including two breaks for coffee and something to eat, and counting again the returning trip out, we would actually work barely full four hours, but were paid for eight. That was another good part of the whole deal. No wonder that the regular soldiers would call us, "Blackies", the "Black Barons"! Well, we sure looked like ones after the shift. The coal dust stuck to our bare, wet and perspiring skin (we would work only in our undershorts, gloves and helmet), it would get into our eyes, nose and ears, so when we hit the showers after work, only our eyes and teeth would be white. For some reason we could not wash-off the coal dust from under the eyelids, so we constantly looked like having black liners around our eyes.

Anyway, back to my first job. I was assigned to the secondary tunnel to operate a transporter consisting of a compressed air motor driven spool of a long steel cable with a hook on its end. My duty was to give a signal to the other guy down the tunnel who would attach a steel wagon full of steel supports for supporting the ceiling after the coal was removed. The supporting had to be done immediately, as the work progressed, to avoid the tremendous pressure of the above layers to prevent the "ceiling" crush in and bury us all there alive. In those narrow veins we would use adjustable steel supports, while in the tall veins miners would use wooden supports. After receiving the other guy's signal, I would start the spool and pull the wagon in, unhook and unload it and re-hook it back to the cable again. After signaling that the wagon is on its way back and reversing the spool I would watch it disappear slowly into the night. The empty wagon would go down by its own weight and the process would go on and on. It was a great, physically not exhausting job, but a lonely one. After about a week I noticed that every time I was about to take my snack, a mouse would appear! I'm not kidding! A mouse at the 2,800 feet depth! Of course, I shared my snack with it, and we kept company throughout the rest of my work at that station.

After a month I was reassigned to the party that was supposed to make the main, large tunnel longer into the continuous coal field. Now here's how this racket worked.

As I mentioned before, the coal mining was a very important part of the Eastern Block Communist Countries industrial output. Therefore special, preferred groups of dedicated Communist miners were formed. These groups would get a lot of praise and good reviews in local and statewide media who would chart their progress in building the main tunnel on a daily basis. They would be paid very high wages for the each foot tunnel extension.

Now this was a very hard work, indeed. Often the main tunnel had to be dug not only in the brittle coal layer, but had to be extended up or down into the top or bottom layer consisting mainly of solid rock. This rock had to be removed by blasting it off using potent explosives. Very dangerous work, too. Coal mines often are permeated by methane gas which, when ignited, would cause a tremendous blow-out. Also, a certain mixture of fine coal dust and air becomes explosive when ignited by even a spark. That's why all the machinery in the mine was compressed air driven, no combustion engine was allowed. Of course, when blasting, there are sparks, a lot of them! So, the quality of surrounding air had to be constantly monitored, especially where blasting occurs.

The rocky "forehead" of the tunnel had to be drilled some 4 feet deep in many places, stuffed with explosives and blasting caps that would be wired to a main blasting station. All that had to be covered over with special stuffing material, so the force of the blast would have to work against the rock, and sparking would be prevented. After all the stuffing was done, all workers had to retrieve in special shelters back in the tunnel during the blast. A special signal sounded and after that a tremendous blast, which, in those confined places would be really an ear popping one, occurred. We all had to wear special ear muffs during this. After a while when the noxious fumes dissipated in constant air flow, we would all go back and started to load the blasted-off rocks into carts. The shape of the tunnel had to be somewhat smoothed to conform to the plan, and immediately supported by 1 x 3 feet and some 3 inches thick concrete boards held in place by three piece heavy steel supports, consisting of two "legs" and a "top" screwed onto the legs. There would be one, sometimes, rarely, two blasts to a shift.

Now here comes the trick. In the media there was no mentioning about the fact that at least one, sometimes even two shifts were actually worked by the Black Barons. The specially formed groups, named for a famed Soviet miner Stachanov (no doubt that he achieved his progress by similar means) competed against each other, and were paid for a total progress, done by a large part by us! This was typical for the smoke-and-mirrors Socialist economy that had to show greater productivity than the "Capitalist blood-sucking" one.

I remember one instant while I was working on that job. After blasting, the jagged ceiling had to be smoothed down for the boards and support. I was supposed to pick-off a large boulder protruding from the ceiling down. I had to stand on another, wobbly boulder standing just under the one I was supposed to remove. Now, I was about 5 feet 9 inches, some 140#, no heavy fighter. To get that boulder off the ceiling I had to use some 30 lbs heavy

JUST ANOTHER ORDINARY LIFE

compressed air driven pick that would rapidly pound into the stone, not unlike a machine gun. I had to hold the pick in my hands up, over my head. As I was poking into the boulder, my pick suddenly slipped over the slick surface and weight of the machine pulled me forward. To balance and prevent my fall off the stone I was standing on, I immediately bended backwards. At that instant, just as I was bending back, that darned, couple of hundred pounds heavy boulder got loose from the ceiling and crashed down right in front of my retracting face! A split second saved my life....

I was not good for work for the rest of my shift.

After couple of months, I was re-directed to the actual coal extracting shift. There were ten pairs of us working on the entire some 300 feet long coal vein, each having about 30 feet segment.

The graveyard shift, before our shift came in, moved the narrow conveyor belt closer to the coal wall, leaving about 3 feet space between them. They would also move pipes for compressed air in similar fashion. The dug-out empty space would be filled up by dirt and gravel after the steel supports were pulled out. This was a very dangerous job, since in those 18 hours of coal extracting tremendous pressure continued to work on the ceiling. It often happened that after the steel supports were pulled out (by special pullers using very strong cables) the ceiling would collapse before the graveyard shift guys were able to fill the empty space with dirt. That's why, in mining regions, often one could see sudden dips on roads, fields and even in villages, as these collapses would eventually transform the upper ground surface.

We had to crawl to our work place (remember, the vein was just about 4 feet thick), lay on our sides or backs, grab somewhat smaller picks and start poking them into the coal wall. The other guy, armed with a short handle shovel, would pick the fallen down coal and move it over his stomach onto the running conveyor belt. In a while we would switch places. As soon as we extracted some

2 feet of coal, we would have to place the steel supports to make sure that we would not be buried in there. Each shift was able to extract about 3 feet of coal alongside the 30 foot wall, so the entire segment moved closer to the main tunnel by about 6 feet every day. And so it went, day after day, with only Sunday, and occasional Saturday rest.

Of course, when we finally emerged from the deep out, showered and changed into our uniforms again, we were all thirsty. It took about an hour to get the whole shift ready for transport back to barracks. Usually, we would go to a nearby pub and have some good Czech beer. There were some amongst us who would order "a meter of beer", that means 9 half liters (about 18 oz), and were able to gulp them down. Well, you can imagine how the return trip "home" looked like. Funny thing, though, we were "soldiers", but the brass never complained, as long as we did our part in the mines......

During my entire year in the coal mine I did not go home or Liberec to see anyone of my family, not even for a single day.

Sundays would be dedicated to "the day on the town". We had a good group of guys in our bedroom, so we would generally go out together, went dancing (this time the girls didn't mind - was it because we did have money?), went swimming or girl watching into a park. Sometimes we would take a short train ride to Ostrava's surroundings, full of beautiful green meadows and fields. Laying on our backs, watching the clouds go by, and just to try to get some fresh air into our with coal dust filled lungs. Good thing that I never smoked!

While all this was going on, the company my Father worked for changed it's name and was regrouped. As a part of the reorganization my Father moved to Krasna Lipa, where he was taking care of the dye house, together with other two dyehouses in different cities that were now part of the new company. As a part of the deal, the company let him stay in a small house with a nice yard, garage and a flat roof, all painted pink, but without having paying rent. Pavel, of course, moved there with my father, too, and subsequently decided that he will become a textile dyer also!

As it happened, the Dvur Kralove textile dyeing school (the one i once attended) was full, but there was an opening in a textile dyeing school in Krnov in Northern Moravia. Krnov was not too far from Ostrava, some two hours of train ride with one change of train on the way. Pavel and I were in touch by mail so one nice late-fall day of 1956 I decided to take a trip to Krnov to see him.

Little did I know that this trip was going to change my life entirely.

Marta.

The train stopped at the old Krnov train station and belched dark smoke to say good-bye to me.

I asked the station attendant for directions to the school Pavel was attending and living in for two years. This school, just like my old one in Dvur Kralove, was also organized and ran similarly. Three days of schooling, three days of practical work in a dye house per week. The students would be housed in separate buildings, some for boys, others for girls, with the 24/7 supervision over them.

It was a sunny and mild Sunday, almost noon time, when I rang the bell at the dormitory entrance. A lady opened the door for me, and after my asking for Pavel, she declared that she would fetch Pavel's housemother, a lady who would be directly responsible for him. After a phone call and a short waiting this lady appeared, all smiles. She was very pretty, about my age and little shorter than I, not thin and not overweighted, with full head of dark brown hair and pronounced dark eyebrows over soft and smiling blue eyes. She wore a little make-up, but not too much, just to emphasize her full red lips.

I introduced myself politely and she said that she was Miss Marta Kuntscherova, Pavel's housemother. We chatted a little bit and it was obvious to me that she new our family circumstance. That didn't bother her, opposite, I got an impression that she sympathized with Pavel for that. She than took me in Pavel's room which he shared with three other boys to meet him. Pavel was in the room alone, the other boys were gone to their families for the weekend. Pavel and I didn't see each other for quite some time, so our meeting was a very nice and noisy one. We embraced and Miss Kuntcherova left us alone. Before she departed, she invited me to a lunch with Pavel in the school cantina, though. That was very appreciated by me which I expressed fondly.

Pavel and I spent some three hours together with Miss Kuntcherova appearing from time-to-time and adding to our conversation about Pavel's progress at school, his behavior and such. She did not have any complaints which I was glad to hear. Pavel was able to go with me to the station and wave good-bye to me as I was waving back to him from the departing train window.

I had plenty of time to think on my way back to Karvinna about Pavel and his school. I liked it. In those days it was not easy to live anyplace with the fact that both of your parents were or are in prison for political problems, so I could appreciate Miss Kuntcherova interest in Pavel and her being somewhat protective of him. In the eyes of some zealous Communist boss her stance could actually harm her carrier.

I liked her. I liked her a lot! So much so that in my next letter to Pavel I asked him to try to get and send me her photograph. Pavel's next letter to me was only full of scorn about my wish. He was describing how hard he tried to get Miss Kuntcherova picture for me, but to no avail. Only much later I learned that nothing of that was true, that he simply approached Miss Kuntcherova and asked her for a picture, declaring: "That idiot of my brother wants your picture, Miss, could you, please tell me where on Earth could I come across one for him?" Well, that was Pavel's refined diplomacy! It didn't work either. Even much more later I learned additional particulars of my first visit to Krnov. As it happened, Pavel, because he was already working for some time, he was the oldest boy in that school year. He was of similar stature as I, so he would wear much of my clothes there, including then "modern" loud ties with fist-size knots, very narrow-legged pants (in some cases we would have to have a zipper put in the bottom of the pants legs in order to be able to pull them on) and shoes. When Miss Kuntcherova would ask him where, for crying out loud, he got these things, he would proudly say: "From my older brother Mirek". So when Miss Kuntcherova learned that I was to come to visit Pavel, she said to her co-workers that she is really very curious about me, and that she was going to talk to me about Pavel's clothes which did not conform well with the spirit of the school. When she came back from seeing me, her co-workers asked her what kind of hell she gave me? She laid down on a couch and started to laugh, saying that I was nothing what she perceived, that I was polite and bashful, nice guy.

The next time I went to visit Pavel it was by the end of November. After arriving to the dormitory, I learned that Pavel's whole class is taking a trip to Opava to see an ice-skating show. As it happened, there was one more ticket available, and if I'd like, I could go with them. Of course I liked! Actually, it was a very nice show, bettered by the fact that I could sit between Pavel and Miss Kuntcherova, which gave me the chance of talking to her some more. Since my returning trip to Karvina was through Opava anyway, I did not go back with them to Krnov, but rather continued to Karvina with my head full of pleasant memories.

The Christmas was for me just a fleeting moment amidst the work and a little bit of free time that was scarce, as we were asked to go and work on Saturdays and Sundays for the whole of December. For no extra bonus, though, just the straight hours pay. Lots of my buddies went home for vacations and so did Pavel, but I stayed. A book store brought a lot of books in the building for a display and sale. I remember buying a very nicely illustrated Czech translation of Geoffry Chaucer's The Canterbury Tales which I inscribed :"To myself". I enjoyed reading it very much.

I also did find a little free time and courage to write a letter to Miss Kuntcherova to Krnov. Since I got a favorable reply from her, I suggested that we could meet someplace and to know each other better. She suggested Opava. That suited me just fine, since I knew the town pretty well.

So, on the second Sunday in January, around two o'clock we met at the train station in Opava. I felt certain closeness toward her, and was imagining that she felt the same way, as we started to talk easily. We went for a stroll and finally ended in pretty fancy establishment, called Orient for an afternoon tea dance.

We had a very good time, laughing, dancing and talking. I ordered a bottle of wine which was much more expensive than I anticipated, so after paying for the entrance fees, some food and wine, I was left broke. That bothered me, since I had to buy my return train ticket back to Karvina and I knew that I will have to ask Marta (we were on the first name basis by now) to lend me some money for that. It bothered me greatly since I always made sure that I would have extra money on me. It bothered me so much, that I did not dare to kiss her when she came with me to the station in the evening. What an embarrassing situation to be on the first date and having to ask for money! Finally, humiliated, I asked her for the lone which she, laughing, gladly gave to me....

So from now on my monthly trips to Krnov were to see Pavel, but mainly to see Marta. It had to be always on Sundays when she was not so busy, as lots of local boys would go home for the weekend. On one of our meetings Pavel told me that he wanted to take lessons to learn German, but was forbidden to do it! I asked Marta about that and she explained that the school allows learning only

Russian, as it was a part of regular curriculum. No "west" foreign languages were allowed to be learned, even if Pavel would get some private lessons! The school would simply not give him free time to go to these lessons. It was just another example how the Communist regime controlled every aspect of our lives.

For Easter vacation everybody from Pavel's school would go home and Marta would be completely free for two days. She suggested for me to come over on Saturday and stay till Sunday which, of course, I gladly did. Marta and I have had a wonderful time. I still remember marveling about the ceiling in her (provided by the company) room that was all painted sky blue and full of golden stars. Simply heavenly!

Marta was born in 1935 in a little village, Jesenik nad Odrou in Northern Moravia, not too far from Ostrava. Before the World War II the village was predominantly occupied by people with German ancestry. Almost everybody was one way or the other tied to farming. Marta's Father, Johann Kuntscher was also of German descent and being a butcher, but could not bear to slaughter any live animal operated instead the one man village livestock trading business. Later on, he was employed as a border patrol man. Marta did not have many memories of him, since he had to go to the War when she went the first day to school in 1941. Johann came home few times for a brief vacation during the war. After the war ended Johann did not return from it as he was in 1944 declared Missing In Action on the eastern Russian front. Few years later there was a rumor that he has been seen in some remote Russian village, but that was never confirmed. In any case Marta and her a year younger sister Olga were raised only by their Mother Anezka, born Myslikovjanova a lady of Czech descent. Marta's family and her father's mother lived in a small rented house without electricity and a small property around it, that enabled them to keep a cow, goat, gees and chickens all of which was very important for survival during the war. There also was a small vegetable garden there. Marta's mother would also go and help neighboring farmers at the time of harvests for a trade of grain, potatoes and such which helped her to keep all the animals. Often Marta and Olga would go and help too.

Because the girls were from a mixed marriage (in Europe the descendancy plays an important role) people in the village would not treat them kindly. During the war they both had to go to German school (that part of Czechoslovakia was in Sudetenland), but at home they were speaking Czech with their Mother. After the war they did not have to go to Germany because of Anezka's Czech origin. To establish that took some time, and until that was done they all had to wear a wide yellow banner on their sleeve with a large black N (for Nemec = German in Czech) on it, making them automatically an outcast and causing the girls a lot of grief. Even at school some teachers would not treat them kindly! In a strange way, I felt very close to Marta, as Pavel's and mine situation right then was actually similar. We, too, were marked.

When the German population had to leave Czechoslovakia for Germany after the war (including Marta's father family), a lot of Czech newcomers came to Marta's village. Anezka was able to get a job as a cook in a large flour mill some three miles distant from the village and the school. Those were hard times for both girls. They had to walk to school by foot every day, sun, rain or snow. After school they had responsibilities to help with keeping their household (that was in the flour mill now) in order, and sometimes even in the kitchen where their mother worked for the whole day preparing all the meals for some 70 employees there.

After the grammar school Marta and Olga had to take train to go to the high school. The train station was also some three miles away from their home. Understandingly there was not too much money in the family. Colleges were far away, and to secure an apartment and books was costly. Olga was regarded as the brighter one from the two sisters, so Marta persuaded her mother that it should be Olga who would go on to college when the time comes. After the high school Marta went to live with her married cousin Herta in Opava to attend two-year long trade school there to become a professional photographer. A year later Olga went to Prerov, a large city in the region, to attend the College of Chemistry. Despite many disadvantages and hardship in their lives, both sisters retained an upbeat outlook on the life. When both girls were out of the house, Marta's mother remarried. Her new husband Julin Machycek was by eleven years younger and worked with the railroad company. To earn more money to keep Olga at school Anezka went to manage and cook in the village pub and restaurant. It was a very hard work, as a lot of the villagers would come for lunch just about every day. The week-ends were especially hard since often there was a dance on Saturdays. Marta would come home on these occasions and help mother with cleaning the restaurant and the ball-room after that.

One day coming back home for the week-end Olga waited for Marta at the train station. "Guess what!" she said and proceeded to tell Marta that their mother was pregnant! Both girls were quite concerned about the news as their mother was already 46 years old. Luckily everything went well with the pregnancy and on the first of April 1955 a baby girl Dobruska was born. Until now all three girls are maintaining a very good relationship and are close to each other.

After finishing her schooling with honors Marta started to work at a photo studio as an apprentice, and later on was able to take pictures, develop films, print and enlarge photographs and anything that came her way by herself. Eventually she became a manager of the studio, but because of the low pay she decided to change jobs. The local work department found her a job as a quality controller in the safety razor producing company. That was an easy, not frustrating job, but she had to work the graveyard shift, as the company, just like most of other companies, was running a three shift operation. She lasted there for about six months, but the in-the-middle of night everyday walk to work was, for a young woman not too safe a proposition. After that she worked for about a year as a book-keeper at a scrap metal company before finally landing the job of house-mother in Krnov, eventually taking care of Pavel and thus meeting me.

Marta and I kept meeting more frequently now and in about a month she took me to meet her mother whom I liked right from the start. She was very kind, pleasantly plump with a crown of white hair over her pretty face. I believe that she liked me as well. I learned later that after Marta questioned her about me, she replied: "Yes, I like him, but he is such a boy!" I guess not even my uniform could better my boyish look. At another time Marta took me to meet her aunt Mila in Budisov a town in a hilly and wooded country. Aunt Mila was a widow with two adult children, a girl Eva and son Draha. Draha left Czechoslovakia right after the 1948 Communist take-over and emigrated via Germany, where he married another Czech emigree Zdena, to Australia and they with their two children finally settled in California. Aunt Mila insisted to prepare a snack for us and wanted to make scrambled eggs with mushrooms. Marta cautioned her that I do not like mushrooms, to which I, ever so polite, replied that no, I will eat them! I did manage (with difficulties) to eat them to Aunt Mila's enormous happiness. "See, he loved them!" she exclaimed and proceeded to make for our lunch a mushroom soup which, unfortunately I just couldn't swallow any more. The whole episode taught me that one should not say what is against his feelings.....

After that Easter we started seriously thinking about our relationship. My tour of duty would end at the fall, and I would be moving back to Krasna Lipa to my old job and to be close to my father again, so Marta decided that she has to be closer to me after that happens. Through a friend she found out that a book printing trade school in Liberec in Northern Bohemia, where babka and my aunts lived, is looking for a house-mother. She did not waste any time and in the summer of 1957 took a trip to Liberec, firstly to see my part of the family there and secondly to inquire about the job. She was satisfied on both fronts, and by the end of summer, just before the school would start, she moved to Liberec and rented an apartment in a house next to the one my aunt Jara and her family lived.

Babka and aunt Jara's family took her under their wings, and she had a very nice relationship with all of them ever since.

All that time I kept in touch with my mom in prison by writing informative letters to her about every aspect of my changing life, but I did miss the personal touch we would always have in the past.

Marta gave her notice in Krnov, but stayed for another month there. At that time Pavel's school offered lessons in parachute jumping through a local paramilitary club. He finished only two sessions out of about ten when another group was ready to perform their first jumps. On the spur of the moment Pavel clandestinely joined the other group, when they boarded the plane, using his parachute. When people started jumping one by one, Pavel just mixed in and also jumped. Later he confessed to us that he was scared to death, but there was no escape as, if discovered, there would be unpleasant consequences for him. Luckily his jump turned out to be a good one and he now had something to brag about. Yes, typically Pavel!

My honorable discharge from the military duty was without a problem, so in the fall of 1957 I was back at my job in Krasna Lipa. Marta now worked in Liberec, some two hours train drive away, and liked her new job very much. We did not have a telephone, so we had to keep in touch only by letter or by taking the train. If I would be coming to Liberec, I would stay with babka in her apartment, but spent rest of the time with Marta. One morning, when I returned back to babka's she told me: "Mirek, I know that you are not going to Marta to pray, but it's not appropriate to stay there over night!" Well, she was from the old school, poor dear.....

When Marta would come to see me in Krasna Lipa, she would stay with me and my father in our rented house. My father liked Marta very much and she liked him, too. Sometimes we would even go for a dance all together or take a hike to the beautiful hilly and green Krasna Lipa surroundings. I again joined the town chess club and the local drama troupe. One nice spring Sunday I was supposed to play chess in a distant town representing Krasna Lipa in a tournament. Marta decided to go with me. We had to take the train for an over an hour journey there. After arriving I had to go inside to the club to play and Marta stayed outside in a park thinking that I will be back in an hour or so. Unfortunately, the game kept dragging on, and even though I had a winning position, my opponent was a good one and I could not finish it soon enough for Marta. Finally, she decided to come in and announce to me that she was leaving in order to catch the next train back! And she did just that! Now, what was I supposed to do?!? I tried to successfully finish my game, but could not in time, so I offered the draw which, of course was promptly accepted. After shaking hands, I started to run to the train station and got there just in the nick of time when the station master was just about to give signal for the train to leave! Well, I made OK with Marta, but the members of my chess club stopped to greet her from now on. At another time my drama troupe had an engagement in the neighboring town performing sort of a cabaret. After that there was a dance. Marta was never keen on my acting, being in company of other young females. She was far from being a prude, she just had strong feelings for what is appropriate and what is not. Marta came over from Liberec and I told her about the dance, conveniently leaving the cabaret unmentioned. My father would also accompany us. Marta agreed, we got into a train and went for the dance. After arriving there she, of course, found out about the cabaret, too. She grudgingly accepted the fact and took her seat beside my father. One of the skits I was involved in was set in a park. On a park bench three old gentlemen, a school teacher, a priest and a policeman (I was the teacher) sat and were discussing how immoral the youth nowaday is. Suddenly a beautiful girl in a mini skirt appears and parades in front of them swinging her behind across the scene. All three oldies, their eyes bulging kept staring and turning their heads after her as she walked by. When she disappeared, all three of them, in unison said: "Boy, what a beautiful ass!"

As the whole room was laughing and clapping, Marta stood up and marched right out. My father, bewildered, following her. I stood on the scene, bowing to the crowd. Finally, I realized what was happening and was starting to get angry. After a while, though, I excused myself and went after them. I found them on the train station, Marta fuming and my father consoling her. I tried to talk to Marta, but she refused to talk to me. In a while my father calmed her down and told me that it looks like I will have to make my mind and choose between the drama club and Marta. Luckily, I did the right thing and promised her that I am going to quit the drama club. The crisis was averted and my lifelong commitment to Marta confirmed.

The next day Marta and I had a long talk and agreed that we should get married.

JUST ANOTHER ORDINARY LIFE

From the top down:

The back side of the house we bought together with my father. It's the same house I rented a room in just few years ago.
Our living room there.
Any chance we got we would take trips into our near surroundings.

Miroslav Kolias

Clockwise from the top:

Marta at the time I first met her, 1956.
Marta's mon Anezka with Marta and Olga, cca 1941.
Marta's father Johann Kuntscher as a German soldier at home, cca 1943.
Marta's mom when she learned that her husband is MIA, 1944.
Marta's first communion, cca 1943.
Marta with sister Olga, 1955.
Marta in 1956.

The third beginning.

As it happened, my co-worker was about to move to a different city, putting his house up for sale. It was the same house I used to rent a room in when I first came to Krasna Lipa! I knew the house well, a large, two story place with a veranda and balcony over it, almost fully cellared and sitting in a very large garden full of fruit trees, large spruce trees alongside the farthest property line, a greenhouse, a little swimming pool and lots of red and black currant, raspberry and blackberry bushes. It would be ideal for two families living together, yet having plenty of privacy for each of them.

I talked it over with my father (who approved of my marrying Marta wholeheartedly), so we went to take a look at the house and talk to Jan right away. Without delay we agreed on his terms. In couple of days, we all went to the Notary in nearby Rumburk, our county seat at that time, gave Jan some 15,000 Czech Krowns and received our Deed of Trust in return. I was making some 1,500 CK a month, so the price for such a house was a very good one indeed. My father and I would each put a half of the money up, but my father suggested to make the Deed in my name, since I'd inherit his half one day anyway.

As soon as Jan and his family moved out of the house, we moved in. Since the furnishings from our apartment in As has been put in storage by my uncle Pepa after my parents were imprisoned, we had enough to furnish the main, some 450 sq. feet (!) large, downstairs living room, a small downstairs bedroom, downstairs kitchen and upstairs main bedroom, more than enough for the three of us to live there comfortably. As soon as Marta would move from Liberec to Krasna Lipa, Marta and I would take the upstairs bedroom, my father the downstairs one and the kitchen, living room and bathroom would be shared by all of us. After work, when having time (which was seldom) we would all gather in the large living room and watched TV that, at that time, had only two channels available. At least we didn't have to fight about what program to watch, right?

Having a good place to live in, next in order was our marriage. Since Marta's family lived in Moravia, and there was more of them than us, we decided that we would exchange our wows in a civil ceremony in Opava on the 27th of September 1958. At that time living was quite expensive, some 70% of one's salary went for food, so money was rather scarce, therefore only the immediate family would attend our wedding, but the occasion had to be very nice nevertheless. I bought Marta a very nice, square blue topaz engagement ring.

Marta decided (after some nerve wrecking scouring of many fashion magazines for just the right model) to have her silver color two piece dress for the wedding made by a seamstress in Rumburk, a special white hat, modeled somewhat after a leaf of the beautiful Liriodendron Tulipifera tree growing in the local park, was also ordered to be made, and I had to go and buy me a new suit, announcements of our Big Day were ordered, and so on, and so on. We asked Marta's sister Olga and my cousin Ernstik to be witnesses to our getting together forever. They both accepted happily. Other guests were Marta's mother and stepfather with their daughter Dobruska, Marta's cousin Herta with husband Arnost and their children Rudi and Eva and from my side my father, my brother Pavel, aunt Ela and her son Ernstik.

The last night before the wedding Marta and my side of family slept in Herta's house in Opava, and I with Arnost and Rudi slept in their summer house in nearby Komarov. In the morning Arnost had great difficulties to start his VW Beatle to get us to Opava, so I started to run to the bus station hoping to catch a bus there. The Beatle changed its mind, though and started up, so we made it to Opava with about 45 minutes to spare. When I was dressing, Marta discovered that, instead of a regular tie, I packed a bow to go with my suit.

"No way!" she exclaimed. "You'd look like a waiter" and she ran out in her wedding dress to buy me a proper tie. She succeeded, so we were able to come, somewhat winded, to the centuries old City Hall and be "joined together, till death us part" by a frocked City Clerk. Our signatures, as well as Olga's and Ernstik's, attest to that.

A very nice lunch, paid for by my father, followed in the Koruna Hotel on the main square, to which we also invited our taxi driver, so we avoided being the unlucky thirteen of us around the table. After the lunch we all went to Arnost and Herta's house where additional friends of family came to continue the celebration of our happiness. Marta and I left the room a little bit early, just after the dessert, and went dancing for a while before retiring to Herta's bedroom for the night.

Next day, on our way back home to Krasna Lipa Marta and I stopped in Pardubice to visit my mother in her prison, and give her our orchid wedding bouquet. We were able to see her without having first ask for permission long time ahead as customary, because of the special occasion. My mother gave us her blessings and a small apricot tree she grew from a pit in a mug. Tearful good-by followed and we were on our way to our future together.

When back in our new home my father planted the apricot tree in front of the veranda. Krasna Lipa is some 1,500 feet high and in the four season country. Sometimes we'd have over three feet of snow in winter there. Well, despite that the apricot tree kept growing and in few years we were able to pick apricots by just walking out on the balcony. They were very good, too!

I remember that on the first night of Marta's coming back from work at around eleven at night by train, I did not wait for her at the railroad station and went to bed instead, since I had, at that time, to be at work at six in the morning. Anyway, I hear occasionally about that even up to today....

At just about that time Pavel came back home from school in Krnov and got a job in the same company as I did, working in the yarn dyeing division. So, Marta, the newlywed had three men to take care of, to cook and do laundry for us all. We only had a washing machine which did not extract water from the washed clothes. I helped as much as I could, but it was still hard on Marta. After some time, we bought a little free standing electric extractor which was a big help, as on the outdoor line hanging clothes dried much faster. We were happy, though and got along well.

In few months Marta and I also bought a nice, modern oak furniture for the upstairs living room, the one having door out to the balcony. To get a loan was quite impossible at those days, so anything we wanted we had to save for first, so it was a slow going. The furniture consisted of a dining table with four chairs, two bookcases, a case to store beddings in and put a vase on, a coffee table with two upholstered arm chairs and a double bed futon. The wooden floor we covered with wall-to-wall carpet made of about a square foot pieces of some special, tightly woven straw mats sewn together. Two large windows on each side of the balcony door we covered by patterned, bright colored curtains sewn from flat fabric, hanging on a curtain rod running alongside the whole outer wall. We loved the brightness and sunny airiness of that room.

In winter time this, and every other room in the house, were heated by a coal burning, free standing stoves. All the cooking was also done on a coal burning stove. It was quite a chore to keep all the rooms warm in winter. If we were lucky, we'd get a truckload of coal before winter, that was dumped in front of a small cellar window. Myself, Pavel and my father would take turns shoveling it in. Sometimes I had to pull a sled up the hill to the train station and get only the allowable amount of 200 lbs of coal at a time when there was a shortage of it. That, of course, didn't last for too long, and I had to repeat my trips, being glad that the full load I could steer, at least partially, down the slope.

Sometimes at that time Pavel had to go for his army service duty. Originally, he was drafted to the south of Bohemia, very close to the border with West Germany. After about a week working on very secret rocket installations, somebody at his unit HQ found out that he is from the not "secure" family, and got marching orders to move to northern Slovakia. So he packed his belongings, got his rifle and boarded a train, not to Slovakia, but home to Krasna Lipa! If he was caught, he would be court-martialed and spent many years in a prison. Luckily, nobody got wise of his trip, and after spending a day with us he continued to his new destination in Slovakia. For the next two years he worked in his barracks boiler room and have had a good time doing it. Marta's sister Olga, stationed in Slovakia also after her chemistry school, visited him there several times. After the end of his two year duty he got a better job in a textile factory in Chrastava. He moved in with aunt Bozka and uncle Victor there again. He started to date a girl working in the dye lab, and pretty soon he married her. Ladka was from Brno, the largest city in Moravia, where, too, were wool dye houses. Pavel got a job there as a head dyer, and moved to live with Ladka's parents. Soon after their only child, son Peter was born. Unfortunately, Pavel's marriage to Ladka didn't last too long (not by Pavel's fault) and they got a divorce, leaving the baby in the care of Ladka and her family.

All this time Marta worked as a house mother for nursing school that housed its students in a large house in Rumburk. She had to take a train there, and walk about couple of miles from the train station to her job. Usually, she'd go there in the morning, stay working all day and night and got home the next day in the evening. It happened few times that the train from Rumburk would not run in winter for too much of fresh snow on tracks, so Marta had to walk those some 5 miles back home alone at night. It was not possible on our salary to buy and maintain a car, especially when we had to put just about every extra money we'd scrape together in the upkeep of the house and garden. Just about all the work around that house (and it was constant work) I had to do. My father helped as much as he could, but he was getting older, so his responsibility was mainly the garden hot house and a bunch of rabbits we grew to have some meat without standing for hours in line at the butcher's shop. There was shortage of practically everything at those days.

I remember, for example, how hard it was to get an electric hot water boiler for our shower. Like every stove in the house, the bathroom hot water supply was through a coal burning tank, making it very difficult to take a shower every day, especially when the work-day started at 6 AM at the factory. So, we were lucky to get one to two hot showers a week, just like everybody else in the country. Anyway, I asked the company car driver to, please, look out for a boiler for us in places he would go, and had to wait for the brass to end their get-togethers. It took him three months before he located one and another month to get it installed! What a great difference that made to our daily lives!

Our life together was a simple, but a happy one. Marta and I could not take any longer vacation, save for one week in Marianske Lazne I got as a reward for a good work from my company. It was a very nice week, all paid for, staying in a large hotel in a beautiful spa town, having all the meals prepared for us and taking long walks into the surrounding woods.

Not too long after that I was promoted to a company quality controller. It was a very good job, not much of a salary rise, but one shift only! The drawback was my frequent trips to the company Headquarters in Teplice for seminars and additional schooling. Sometimes I had to stay over night, which didn't sit very well with Marta. It helped moneywise, though, as I'd got small bonuses for staying overnight apart from home. At about the same time the position of an accountant opened in my company. Marta applied, and got it! Her duties would be to calculate people's salaries, sick-leave payments and travel bonuses for three hundred people. That was great as we would have the same working hours and Marta would be able stay every week-end at home. The job proved to be a paper pushing one, which did not suit Marta well, as she was accustomed to have a lot of interaction with the girls she used to take care of.

In the spring of 1960 Marta discovered that she was pregnant! We were all very happy about the news, and started to prepare for the happy occasion by buying all the things a little newborn might need.

In April of the same year, we got an unexpected visitor. Olga Bartoskova, my mom's long time co-prisoner, came to see us after her release. She was hopeful that my mother might soon follow her. To our extreme delight in May my mother got a presidential pardon for the rest of her sentence and was sent free from prison! In her release order, though, to our great disappointment, there was a clause that she cannot live in the proximity to any border with Germany or Austria! My mother came to visit us for couple of days, and it was decided, that she and Olga will be living in Cerveny Kostelec for now, where the prison bureau found them both a manual job in a textile machines manufacturing company. We were all hopeful that the clause of restricted living will soon be nixed.

Miroslav Kolias

To prepare for my mother's return, Marta and I bought kitchen furniture and furnished the left upstairs room as kitchen and dining room by dividing it partially in two rooms by a six foot wall ending with a board to place fresh plants on. For the dining room portion we bought a table with four chairs and a futon for eventual guest to sleep on. It took several years before my mother was allowed to return to live with us, though.

JUST ANOTHER ORDINARY LIFE

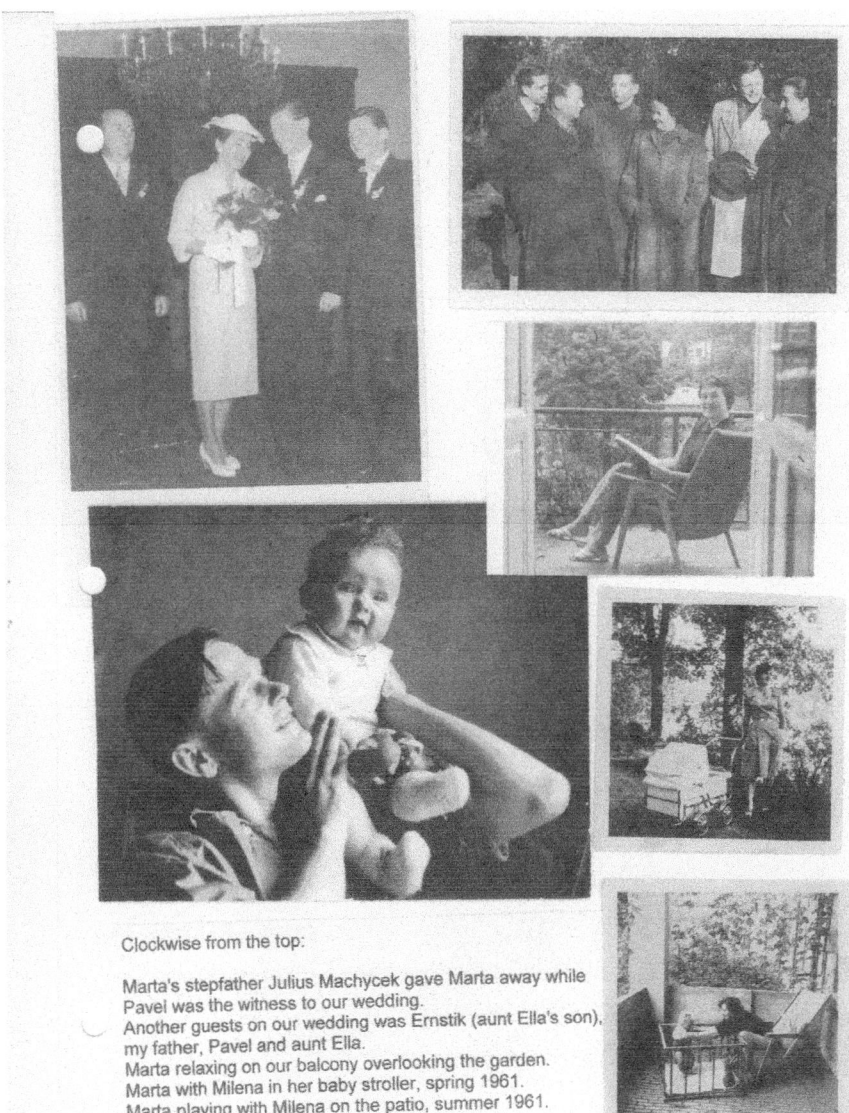

Clockwise from the top:

Marta's stepfather Julius Machycek gave Marta away while Pavel was the witness to our wedding.
Another guests on our wedding was Ernstik (aunt Ella's son), my father, Pavel and aunt Ella.
Marta relaxing on our balcony overlooking the garden.
Marta with Milena in her baby stroller, spring 1961.
Marta playing with Milena on the patio, summer 1961.
So what do you think? Is the future to be OK?

OPAVA, SEPTEMBER 27th 1958

Milena.

In few months Marta was visibly pregnant. Both, Marta's and mine families were very excited and hopeful for a problem free pregnancy and delivery. There was a four month paid leave for expected mothers, so Marta decided to take a month off before her due date.

The morning of November 4th 1960 was rainy and cold when Marta's water broke. My father and I were both at work, so Marta took her already prepared bag with necessary things and went down the street to our neighbor Jana Zeman to ask her to go and let me know, so I could call for an ambulance, since we did not have a phone at home.

Now this was another way of the Communist regime how to make it difficult for people to communicate with each other. We applied for a phone several times, but were always told that there is great shortage of open connecting possibilities and that those few have to be made available for publicly important jobs like teachers, doctors and such. I am sure that our status of the "class enemy" played a significant role for us not to be able to get a phone. To call somebody we would have to go to the post office and use the only town public phone there.

Anyway, Jana came running with the news, the ambulance was called and Marta was moved to the maternity ward at Varnsdorf hospital. Jana told me that Pepa, her husband, could take me to Varnsdorf on his motorcycle later on. Excited and worried at the same time I got a bouquet of flowers, got to Zeman's and behind Pepa on his bike. We made the about 10 miles rainy journey to Varnsdorf, where I joined three other nervous fathers-to-be in the waiting room. I had to wait till 4:30 in the afternoon before a nurse came to show me our beautiful, blue eyed and blond baby girl! She would let me hold the precious, crying new human being for a little while. What a joyous moment! I could not see Marta, though, that was against the hospital regulations, but I was able to leave the flowers for her.

Marta had some delivery problems and had to stay in the hospital for nine days. I still could not come and talk to her. The only way I could see her and our baby was to stand in the courtyard and hope for Marta to see me from her third floor room she shared with eight other mothers. By taking a bus to Varnsdorf I'd come there just about every day. Marta would come to the window and show me our bundle of joy through the glass.

Marta and I decided that if the baby would be a girl, we would name her Milena, after my mother. My mother's name is actually Miloslava, but everybody calls her Milena. When telling that to my mom, she was obviously pleased, but said: "The poor girl is born not only in my sign, but will have my name, too! That might be too much for her to bear!"

When finally, the happy mother and our baby arrived home, we were all elated. Marta proceeded to give Milenka (the diminutive for Milena) her first bath in a little bathtub, bought especially for this occasion and placed on the top of two chairs in the kitchen, when the doorbell rang! Behind the main door stood babka from Liberec, beaming from ear to ear: "I thought that you could use some help!"

she said and took care of her first great grandchild. Marta was actually happy to see babka giving her hand with Milena.

Milena was the apple of our eye and everybody did everything possible to help Marta keep Milena comfortable. Milena would sleep in a crib beside our double bed. She was a very active child, demanding attention by cute "eh-eh-eh" sound, not unlike a chicken call. Marta tried to be the perfect mother, reading a lot about the how and whys around a newborn.

The first snow came by the end of November. Milena was put in a warm sack lined by sheepskin and bundled up so that only her tiny face with bright eyes would be visible. The coal sled now served double duty, taking Milena out with Marta to go proudly to the town. During the day, for Milena's naps after being fed, Marta would take the crib out on the balcony, place Milena in her sack and let her sleep, her face protected, even in the middle of falling snow flakes. I remember the first very cold, crisp, snowy New Year's Eve putting Milena in her sack on the sled and proceed for about two miles to show her to our friends. Perhaps that's why Milena does like coldness in her house now....

After three busy months Marta had to return to her accounting job.

Since we were both working during the day, Marta arranged for an elderly lady, Mrs. Pragerova, to take care of Milena during that time. Marta asked Mrs. Pragerova to feed Milena only the wholesome food, no junk food, no smoked meat, in short just what was good for her. After about a year I remember Marta coming home a little bit early from work and found Milena in town feeding on a smoked beef sausage, smiling happily. That, of course, did not sit well with Marta. Despite that I have to say that Mrs. Pragerova took a very good care of Milena for three years, after which we put Milena to the preschool. Both, Marta and Mrs. Pragerova were sorry for terminating the baby-sitting job, but Mrs. Pragerova stayed in touch with us.

In about two years Marta's previous employer called her if she would be interested coming back to Rumburk as a head of the staff in the boarding school for nursing students. After talking to me we decided that it would be a better job for her, since she never liked the office work very much anyway. Marta would be working only a day shift, but from a solidarity with the other two housemothers, who also had families to take care of, she decided that she would share the week-end duties with them. Thus, every third week Marta would be at work from Saturday noon till Monday morning, leaving me in complete charge of Milena. I guess I did OK since Milena nor Marta ever complained.

My work day started at eight in the morning, so it was up to me to take Milena to the preschool which was in a close proximity to my job. Marta had to take the five o'clock morning train to Rumburk, so she could not take Milena there anyway.

I do not remember one single instant when we would leave Milena in total care of somebody else, except for the time Mrs. Pragerova took care of her. We just loved to be around Milenka, to watch her grow and making progress. In summer we would spend time with Milenka in our garden, her watching butterflies flying from flower-to-flower on the surrounding bushes. Every time possible we'd take Milenka out in a white baby stroller to the woods, fields and meadows around the town. Often, I'd place her on my shoulders, holding her hands in front of my face. She loved that, expressing her pleasure by laughing and kicking her little feet into my chest.

Milenka's first steps happened in the late fall of the next year in our garden. Marta let her go into the outstretched hands of our neighbor, about ten years old Magda who often came over to play with Milenka. After that Mrs. Pragerova, who had a pronounced limp, had a hard time to keep up with Milena every time she let her out of her stroller.

The following summer Pavel (who already got his driver's license) borrowed uncle Victor's small Renault and took us to see my mom in Cerveny Kostelec who was delighted by her granddaughter. After that we continued on our "show-off" trip to Moravia to see Marta's part of the family, who were similarly impressed. Marta and I were in the seventh heaven.

The years went by and Milena was ready to start her education by attending grammar school that was located about half a mile from our house. Since sometimes neither Marta nor me would be home later in the morning to take her, we taught Milena to go to school using the rear door, locking it after herself. The key was supposed to be placed under a bucket standing in the corner of the veranda. Well, first time she did everything right, except for the key which she placed into the bucket for everybody to see! I am happy to say that that mistake was never repeated. It's interesting that we were never afraid of someone harming or snatching Milena on her way to school. One thing the Communist regime achieved was that these sorts of crimes were at their bare minimum. There was almost total control of people and their movements. Every crime was immediately, severely and uncompromisingly punished.

In school Milena did very well. Since she was born in November, she went to the first grade actually being almost seven years old. She was ready to fight to be in the first row for everything. Even the boys could not stop her.

During summers Milena would play in our small pool, often with Hanka, our other neighbor daughter and Magda. When Dobruska from Moravia would come to stay with us, she, too, would happily join them all. The garden was full of happy screams and water fights.

My father arranged for a truckload of fine sand to be brought and placed in a large mound in the back, close to the back door. Milena loved to play in the sand "baking" cup cakes, building fantastic castles and digging deep in the sand. In winter time, when everything would be under some two feet of snow, Milena helped to clear the path to the rabbit coops, chicken plot and our wood pile. They were all at the back of the house, by wooden shack that at one time served as a bee-house.

Rabbits were our meat supply, we'd have some seventy of them every year. It was my job (I hated it) to kill, skin and disgorge them for Marta to prepare excellent meals from. Good meat was hard to come by without standing in long line (sometimes for hours) in front of the butcher shop. Especially her soup was a hand down winner. Chickens, too, were needed as there was likewise a constant shortage of fresh eggs at the market. As it happened, the government issued a directive that anybody who owned a garden large enough (ours was about 1 1/2 acre) and kept chickens, would every month have to bring a certain amount of eggs to the city office to help minimize the shortage. Marta didn't like the idea and said that we are not going to give away any eggs from our measly five chickens. Well, I am not a guy who'd like to fight, especially not a city. So, on a sly, I started to collect some of the eggs to give to the city. Unfortunately, Marta found them. Heated exchange with me followed and I challenged her to go to the city hall and tell them about not giving them any eggs.

"Yes, I'll do just that!" Marta replied and next time the city agricultural commission was in session, she went to attend the meeting. She explained them that we are four people having five chickens and able to consume all the eggs they produce. The commission did not budge and ordered Marta to produce those (I've forgotten how many we were supposed to give them) eggs.

"In that case I'll rather kill the chickens!" Marta said. "You should be happy that we are self supporting in eggs, not to buy them and making the shortage even worse!" "We know that you are not going to kill the chickens, so you have to bring those eggs" was the stern reply of the commission chairman. "You are mistaken, I will kill them!" Marta retorted. "OK, but we will come and check on that!" the chairman said. Well, we did kill the chickens, they came to check them out and from then on, we got our eggs from store, when they were available. It's mind boggling, but that's how the Communist regime operated. Private possession of just about anything was frowned upon.

Nevertheless, Milena kept growing and prospering along just fine, thank you.

Miroslav Kolias

Clockwise from the top:

Summer relaxation, 1961.
Stopping at my mom's in Cerveny Kostelec on the way to Moravia to see Marta's family.
Pavel drove us in Victor's car.
Milena's first step, 1961!
What do we have there?
Our "burgeois" style of life.

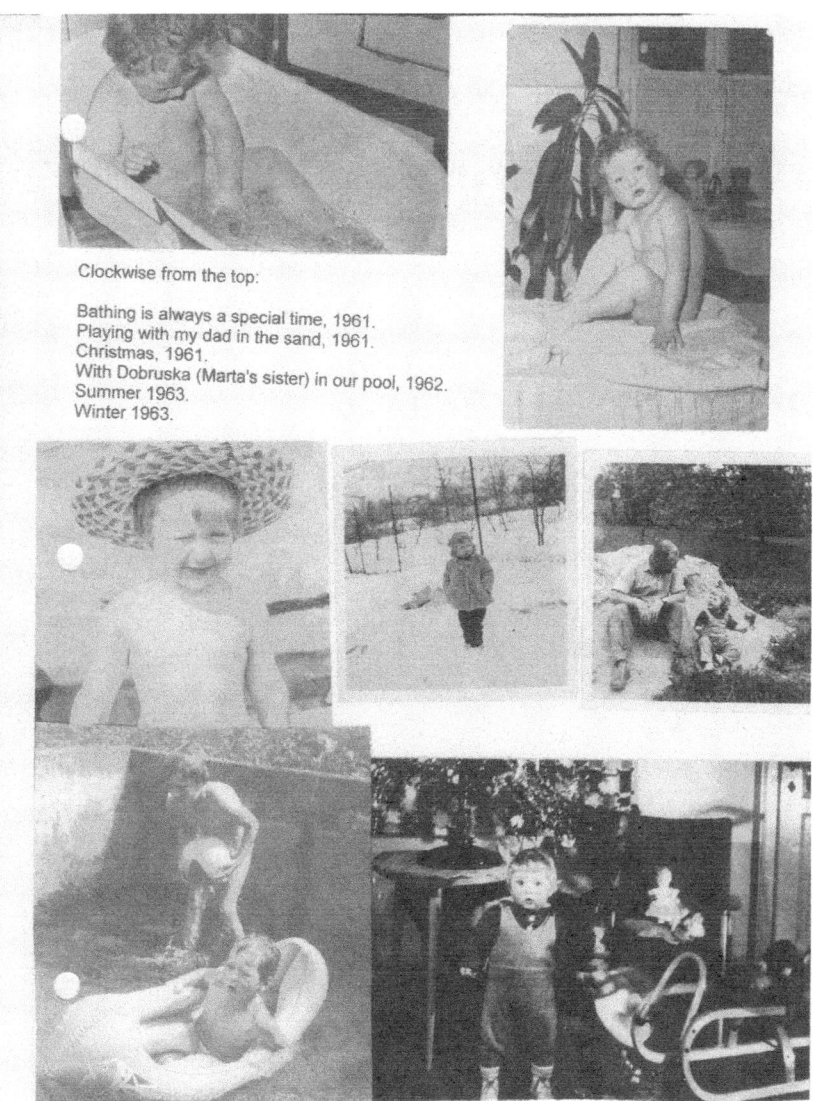

Clockwise from the top:

Bathing is always a special time, 1961.
Playing with my dad in the sand, 1961.
Christmas, 1961.
With Dobruska (Marta's sister) in our pool, 1962.
Summer 1963.
Winter 1963.

Is the real Spring really coming?

From the time Milena was born, for some eight years, several important events occured.

My mom, after several years, was allowed to come to live with us! The whole family was excited and looking forward to that. As my mom's long time companion Olga Bartoskova (my mom credited her with practically saving her life in Pardubice prison) did not have any family left as her mom died recently, it was decided that she would come to live with us, too. My mom got together with my father again, but in a short time their relationship started to deteriorate. The new living arrangements had to be found. Marta, Milena and I kept the upper kitchen and living room, my father got the room downstairs, the one I once rented when first coming to Krasna Lipa, and my mom and Olga occupied the large bedroom upstairs. The downstairs kitchen served to my mom, my dad and Olga as well as the very large living room downstairs. Luckily the size of our house allowed us all to live our separate lives in relative calm and peace. It was difficult for me, though, as I loved both my parents equally, and so did Marta. Milena did not know, or could not understand the situation yet.

My mom and Olga got a job first in Rumburk, and after about a year in the same factory I worked for in Krasna Lipa.

After some regime softening in the late fifties, harsh times came again in early sixties and my father, after refusing to join the Communist Party, lost his textile technician job in our plant. We both were devastated by that and I decided that I, too, will quit my technician job there. My father persuaded me, though, not to do such a foolish thing, especially now, when Marta and I had our child. Reluctantly I saw his point, and stayed on at my job. My father got another job, as a laborer in a nearby town, again in a large textile factory where he worked in a dye storage room weighing and dispensing dyes and chemicals according to given recipes. It was a hard and dirty work, but he did not complain. He only had a couple more years to retirement which he took as soon as he could. Ironically, my factory needed a night watchman right at that time, and my father applied for and got that job. It was an OK job, and helped him with his not too large pension he was getting. On top of that, it was a local job he could walk to. To get to his previous employer at six o'clock in the morning (even though it was only some 8 miles from our house), he'd have to get up at 4 AM, take a train and at the next stop change to a different train on his way there.

Marta's cousin Herta (the one Marta once lived with in Opava) with husband Arnost and kids Rudi and Eva left for a vacation to their distant relatives in West Germany, and did not return back. They left behind all their belongings in Opava. Rudi had finished his architectural schooling already, so all three of them got good jobs in Germany, and reconnected with Herta's family (that was moved as Germans to Germany after the war) there. Herta did not have to accompany them at that time, as she was already married to Arnost. After about two years there they invited Marta, Milena and me to a visit in Wiesbaden. Marta still knew some German, and I was taking private lessons in German language, too, so it should not be a problem for us to stay there also. Unfortunately, we could not get a passport for Milena, as the authorities did not allow any more the whole families to travel abroad, especially not to the "western" world. The government wanted to make sure that the parents would return back as they would not want to leave their children there alone. Talking about being a hostage! Marta and I got our passports, though, and set for our first trip abroad by a train from Prague to Frankfurt, Germany. We had spent a week there and felt like being the Alice in Wonderland, so profound the difference in every aspect of life, compared to our own lives, was there. After coming back, I was called to the local police station where someone (I am sure a secret police member) would interrogate me about our trip in all details. Obviously, I could not tell him my true feelings, so have tried to paint the life there rather bleakly. It was very difficult to do so, as you can imagine.

Again, I decided that I have to finish my schooling in textile technology. I did get permission from my factory director to do so. It meant to get all the books and study materials from the College of Textile Technology in Dvur Kralove, as I'd have to study alone at home, and get there just two times a year for three days, at which time I'd have to do all the examinations for the whole semester from all the subjects. I remembered my failure at the first time I tried, so I decided that this time I have to do it and do it right! Every day after work I'd get into our living room, put some cotton balls in my ears and hit the books for three to four hours. Every day! I was able to persuade Pavel in Brno to do the same. We would do that for four long years, seeing each other in Dvur Kralove at the examinations. Well, we did it, I in Summa cum Laude!

Our factory got a new project to do. We would knit tubular fabric that would have to be washed and bleached, cut into flat form, dried and rolled up into large rolls. The fabric would be the foundation for synthetic leather that would be applied on it by a different company. The final product would be used for garments, both men and ladies like coats, jackets and for upholstery material. It was a very ambitious new product, that nobody else in the country was doing. Our factory director and I got the assignment. We had to design machinery and technology to do it. I am happy to say that we did it very successfully, and actually got a patent on the whole process. At the end it was a very good product, that assured our factory production for many and many years. Incidentally, my mom and Olga, both, worked on the process we invented. Unfortunately, due to the circumstances I will explain later, I never reaped any financial benefit for my efforts.

Shortly after that I was offered a job as a technology specialist at our headquarters in Teplice, a large city famous for its thermal baths. It would be a welcomed job, with much higher salary and a very nice apartment to boot. Marta and I were invited to come to our HQ for a session with the Main Director, who explained me my duties and showed us the great apartment overlooking one of the city main parks. It was a dream job, especially that the situation with my parents at home was getting more and more strung. Of course, I accepted, and agreed to move to Teplice to try it. I'd live for now in an institution that was schooling new employees for the large company sewing department. Everything was arranged, and I left for Teplice in about ten days afterwards. There, at the Technical Directory I got my desk and started to work. The company had three dye houses scattered all over the country, and I was to oversee them all. I liked the job very much. After about a week, when I was already pretty much established there, a man from local Communist Party chapter came to see me. He was curious about how I like the job, the coworkers there and so on. After receiving my satisfactory answers, he offered me to join the Communist Party, handing me some forms to fill-out and return to him. I told him, that I am not very political, that my strength is in technology, and that I don't think of joining in. He expressed his disappointment, and left with the papers in his hand. Well, a week later I was ordered back to my original job in Krasna Lipa, without any explanation!

This was typical Communist regime behavior how to manipulate the Czechoslovak people. If you wanted a good job and good living, you'd have to join the Party and pull its rope. Lots of people, who actually did not agree with the official way (everything was directed through the Communist Party), joined just to better their lives. I just couldn't do that! Of course, I was unhappy, realizing that my knowledge actually does not mean much when it's not supported by my joining the Party. Unfortunately, that's how it was in every aspect of life. In a long run this preference of political ideology over knowledge ultimately brought the total industrial disadvantage and backwardness compared to the Western world. Of course, the peoples living standard reflected just that.

Another, actually larger than the one I was working for, dye house in Rumburk was looking for a technician and offered me a job. I went to see the director who offered me much better conditions of employment. After asking my director for a release from my employment, I was told that he cannot do that, as he would not be able to fill my position with someone else! Yes, that was a provision every employer had. If the employer could not replace someone, he could simply deny the employment termination. A new employer could not employ anyone without previous termination of his or her original job. According to (after the putch of February 1948) the Communist approved new Constitution, everybody was guaranteed a job, but also everybody had to work. Who would not want to work, would end up in a jail and would be assigned some kind, however inconvenient, of a job. To achieve (and boast of) a full employment, strict rules, like the one I was subjected to, had to be applied.

In the mid sixties a new Central Communist Party Committee boss Alexander Dubcek was nominated. Now, Dubcek was schooled in the Soviet Union, but his views were much more open than tunnel-vision views of the old Party guard. His motto was: "The

Communism with a human face". This flew directly in the face of the old thinking where the main motto was: " An individual does not matter, it's the collective gains that matter".

Finally, the population felt that is gaining some breathing room in the constricted environment. People started to be much more politically active, supporting Dubcek's views. Large demonstrations against the very repressing President Novotny sprouted all over the country, mainly in the capital Prague. The Soviet Union, as the supreme leader of the so called Eastern Block, started to be very concerned, as it feared that Czechoslovakia could start on its own path, just like Yugoslavia did successfully some time ago, and Hungary tried, but was brutally crushed. To appease Czechoslovak people, the Soviet bosses agreed with removing Novotny from his post and to replace him with an older, fairly popular General Ludvik Svoboda, a hero of the World War II. It didn't work, people still wanted independence from Soviet Union. Dubcek pressed forward, gaining tremendous support for his changes toward almost total independence. Several strong warnings from the Soviet Union leaders and various government officials followed, culminating with a visit of Soviet President Brezhnev in Czechoslovakia.

Dubcek, feeling the free world support behind him, did not budge and with tremendous accolades from the Czechoslovak people continued with his program. He was convinced that, after the world's hugely negative response to the Hungarian revolution crush, the Soviets would not dare to repeat a similar action.

As time proved, Dubcek's calculations were wrong.

Miroslav Kolias

Clockwise from the top:

Pavel got married to Ladka in Brno.
Books were always an important part of our lives, 1965.
Milena's first wheels! 1965.
We took a trip to see friends in Karlovy Vary, 1965.
My mom with Olga Bartoskova came to live with us, 1965.
On our trip to Germany to see Herta and Arnost (Ernst), 1967

JUST ANOTHER ORDINARY LIFE

Clockwise from the top:

Even Pavel came to help. 1963.
Summer 1963.
Trip to Yugoslavia with uncle Victor and aunt Bozka, 1964.
Jirka was also there.
Jirka is guarding Milena in Dubrovnik, 1964.
Good think that she could help us! Winter 1964.
With neighbour Hanka in summer 1963.

September 21 1968.

At three o'clock in the morning on this fateful day my father knocked on our bedroom door: "Wake up, our country is being occupied!"

He usually got up at that time to get himself ready for the train ride to work. By doing so he would turn on his radio that was tuned to the Radio Free Europe broadcast. That's where he first heard the terrible news. The Soviet, East German, Polish and Hungarian armies crossed the borders of Czechoslovakia to "restore peace and order that were threatened by the Dubcek's revisionists".

The whole country was in shock. The world woke up in disbelief over the brazen Brezhnev action who just couldn't bear that a small country like Czechoslovakia would stand up against his wishes, and tried to chart its own political course. The heart of Europe was attacked from east, north, west and south by powerful armies against which there simply was no possible defense.

Dubcek and his government assessed the situation correctly and declared no armed resistance to the rapidly advancing tanks and heavy guns. Within a day the whole country was occupied.

Soldiers in invading tanks were taken aback by the fact that, contrary to what they were originally told, there was no visible threat present to anyone. In Prague and other large cities people would approach tanks en mass chanting "Go home, let us be!" and pushing flowers into the tank guns openings. Factories stood still, trains, buses and street cars were not running. Everybody was out in the streets and the Czechoslovakian armed forces stayed in their barracks. The incoming soldiers, to their complete amazement, did not have anyone to fight! There was no support of their task to "restore peace" amongst the millions of Czechoslovakia inhabitants.

Without any organized resistance, people just took into action for themselves. In many places town the street name signs disappeared over night causing a complete invader disorientation. The first wave of invading soldiers, who witnessed the untruthfulness of their original situation description in Czechoslovakia and got orders to fight, had to be replaced within two weeks of their arrival with new ones.

People from all over the country kept coming to Prague to protest the invasion. The whole original government was seized by the Soviets and moved to Moscow for "consultations". New government, agreeable to the Soviet "friendly help" came back. Most of the Communist Party members kept throwing their ID cards away. Young student Jan Palach doused himself with gasoline and set himself on fire burning to his death on the main Prague square the Wenceslav's Square. In short everything was in chaos.

Pavel came to visit and announced that he and his fiancee Lida are going out of the country and will try to get to the West. My mother went with them to Yugoslavia where they got married. Through my mom's old acquaintances there, dating back to the World War II, she secured the newlyweds transport to the neighboring Austria and into a refugee camp.

Marta and I were also agreeable to the idea, as we realized that the "Prague Spring" came to a screeching halt and was replaced by a terribly cold and dark winter. Also, the tension between my parents played a part of our decision making. I took advantage of the everlasting chaos, and after spending a whole day standing in line before the Austrian Embassy, was able to receive their six months valid visas for all three of us. Unfortunately, we could not leave right away like Pavel did, as we realized that the house we were all living in (since it was in my name), would be confiscated by the State when we would not return from our trip to Austria and my parents would have to move out. After family discussion it was decided that I will say that my father and I came to an disagreement, and therefore we want the title of the house to be divided back to both of us. That took some time, as it involved paperwork and a notary to sign on it.

While the paperwork was being done, my cousin Eva and her husband Franta came to see us and told us that they, too, want to get out of the country. Since Marta knew pretty well German and since Eva was three months pregnant with their first child, they came to ask, if we would not go with them. We explained them our situation, and it was agreed that as soon as the house paperwork comes through, we all will go together. Marta let her cousin Herta in Germany know about our decision, and she wholeheartedly supported it.

Hopeful good-bye.

While we were waiting for the house papers to be completed, with Marta we constantly talked about our decision and what it will all mean for the whole family. The tension between my parents grew even worse, as much as they practically stopped talking to each other and left written messages to each other on the top of our small refrigerator.

That bothered both of us tremendously and we realized that to raise Milena in this environment would not be too good for her.

Yes, it was the right decision to leave!

Another very unexpected and sad event occurred just at that time. Marta's Mother Anezka died very suddenly. She didn't feel good, went to the hospital for examination, but was told that they could not take her in for lack of place. She went back home and died over night from a blood clot that got to her heart, causing a sudden and deadly heart attack on the 21st. of January.

Marta received a telegram from Olga saying just that.

Right away we got on the train and went to Jesenik. We stayed there for couple of sad days, attended Marta's Mom funeral, told Olga what are we planning to do and with heavy hearts returned back home.

Later on Marta often said that for her it was actually better that her Mom died before we left, because if it would have happened after our departure, Marta would blame herself that her Mom died from the sadness and stress our trip would cause her. Someone once said that life is not a bed of roses....... How true!

Dobruska at that time was just a kid, so Olga took her into her house and raised her up together with daughter Petra like her second child. That was very nice of her and until now they all have a very warm relationship together. Marta for all the time helped Olga financially as much as we could.

The house papers were finally ready, so we started to prepare for our departure seriously. To have at least a little money, we sold our very nice stereo radio and I went to Liberec CEDOK (Czech transport company) to buy our three air tickets to Vienna. Franta and Eva did the same in Ceska Lipa.

Our departure day was February the 14th 1969 in the late afternoon.

Eva and Franta got the tickets also on the same flight.

Marta wrote to Herta in Germany the day of our flight to Vienna.

We couldn't tell Milena what are we doing as she could unwillingly let someone know und thus completely ruined our plan.. So, we told her that we are going to go to Prague to take flight over the city, just for an entertainment. She was looking forward to it very much.

Marta started to pack two very small luggages with just the bare minimums of our clothing and such. I gave her seven of my hand written, about six pages each, hard paper folders containing

Czech songs I liked to sing to pack, too. That's how we were prepared for our life changing journey.......

I arranged with Ernstik in Novy Bor (the only person in our family with a car) to take us out to the Prague airport around noon of the 14th February. Franta and Eva would take a train to Prague and we would meet on the airport. Since Franta and Eva did not know any German, it was very important to them that we would fly all together.

At work I said that I had to go with Marta to see Olga, and got two days off. Since I was at that time working on several important jobs with our customers, in my desk I left instructions how to proceed with them to get the satisfactory results. Well, I always tried to be a responsible and helpful person.

In the morning of the 14th, we would go to the train station (we could see my Mom in a distance standing on the road and just looking at us, without waving) to take a train to Novy Bor where Ernstik would wait for us.

He did, put us in his car and gave us two one Dollar bills he somehow owned, to help us out in Austria.

Our trip to Prague went without a hitch and when Ernstik started to say good-bye to us, Milena told him: "You don't have to say good-bye, we will be back very soon, right after our flight over Prague". Ernstik remembers those words until now.

Once in the airport departing hall, we saw Franta and Eva there, too, but did not get together with them, for not bring any extra attention to us.

Everything seemed to go just fine. About twenty minutes before our boarding time, though, an airline attendant came to us and said, that, unfortunately, we will have to be transferred to the next flight, as an emergency occurred and they had to give one of our seats to someone else!

Can you imagine how we felt? Was it true or did they just somehow found out about our decision not to come back?

In a spur of the moment, I said to him that this is not possible, as someone will be waiting for us in Vienna and take us to our tour. Could we just let Milena sit on our laps? It's just a short flight?!?

The attendant thought about it for a minute, took a look at Milena, being an eight years old child, and agreed with my suggestion!!!!!!

The thump of the rock falling from our hearts had to be herd all over there!

Luckily the rest of our trip to Vienna went without hitch and when landing there we told Milena what was actually going on. I do not think that she completely understood that.

We got together with Franta and Eva, hugged each other and wished all the best to each other.

When walking into the arriving hall, we got another shock!

Herta stood there, waiting for us!

She was able to find out what flight we are taking and decided to come all the way from Germany to help us out in Vienna.

We were completely surprised by this, and Herta was too, since instead of just three, there was five of us!

We greeted each other very warmly and thanked Herta profusely. As it turned out, Herta arranged for us a room in a small hotel. Since now there were more of us, we would have to share that one room for the night. That was OK with us all.

Somehow, we managed to get a little sleep, laying on the floor, leaving beds to Milena and pregnant Eva.

Welcome to the new world!!!!!

Waiting in Austria.

We all woke up to a gloomy overcast morning, in the free world we knew very little about, hungry and practically penny-less.

Anticipating that, our good angel Herta came with bunch of rolls, salami, and coffee, fed us. Paid our overnight bill and found directions to the nearest police station where our small group, lugging bags, arrived after about 30 minute walk. Herta explained the situation to the desk officer there who invited us all in for a talk about our political asylum.

He was mostly interested if we wanted to stay in Austria, or if we plan to go someplace else to live. We told him that we all wanted to stay for only as long as necessary for us to obtain visas to go someplace else. After filling up a bunch of papers and signing them, he took us all to the back yard, where we had to say thanks and good-by to Herta. After teary parting with Herta we all got into a van and were driven for about an hour to Treiskirchen, south of Vienna. During this journey none of us hardly spoke to each other, everybody was preoccupied with his or her inner thoughts.

What is going to happen to us?

Was our decision the right one?

Will we ever be able to go and see our families back home?

Finally, we arrived into the small town of Treiskirchen where a huge 19th century army barracks, three stories high, were standing in their grey overcoats. Large iron gate got opened for our group and an officer escorted us all into an office. Marta's German was sufficient enough to explain our situation and our please for political asylum. After more paperwork we were all taken into another office where we were each given a bar of soap, two metal army issue bowls with handles that fit into each other, eating utensils, a toothbrush and toothpaste, a comb and couple of handkerchiefs. After that we were escorted into one of the large buildings and in a huge, some 15 feet tall room on the first floor. The room was some 20 x 40 feet, with six large windows on the outer side of the building and divided by cables into small partitions. From these cables hung large dark grey blankets separating the "rooms". Each "room" was furnished with two bunk beds, two metal night stands and couple metal chairs and a small metal folding table. Eva and Franta got one of those rooms and Marta, Milena and I got another. There were about 16 partitions like that with an open narrow central walkway in each room. To get into one of the partitions, one just had to pull aside the front hanging blanket and then close it after himself. Every such partition was occupied, mostly by two people. Everything that was said was clearly heard all around, since the top of those partitions were completely open. There were four of such rooms on every floor of those buildings.

The officer who brought us in wished us all good luck, told us that we will be given three meals a day, some pocket money of 35 Shillings per week per family, and that we cannot venture outside of the barrack compound without a special permission obtainable in the office by the iron main gate. The whole compound was enclosed by a 12 foot tall, thick brick wall, and there were sentries present during the night outside. He told us that is is all for our protection, since there were cases in the past that some prominent refugees would be kidnapped by secret service personnel of their original governments and taken back.

On each of the floors there were two main restrooms, one for ladies, one for men, each with a row of open stalls and a row of cold water only wash-basins. Once a week there were hot showers available there. There were no cleaning crews in the buildings, so all the restrooms were in a very sorry stage, with wet floors and dirty stalls. The whole situation was not encouraging.

After lunch was served in our metal bowls after standing in a long line in the mess hall, and eaten sitting on wooden benches by long, bare wooded tables, we all had to wash our bowls and utensils in a large open kettle full of hot water, with oily spots floating on the surface of it. We used our given handkerchiefs to dry the bowls out.

In the afternoon, all the newly arrived (there was a constant stream of new people arriving) men were taken into a different building, up on the third floor. Franta and I were amongst them. We had to take our personal belongings with us and were told that we will be separated from our families for two weeks for a quarantine. We, the men, were placed in an open room full of cots with a little night stand beside them. One by one we were taken into a private room where we would be interrogated by a Czech (or other languages as needed) speaking people. They wanted to know all the details of our lives in our respective countries, what army unit we served in, what was our family life like back home and so on. In those two weeks I was interrogated three times for about two hours at a time. Otherwise, we would be just kept in the room, talking, playing cards or reading. In the evening we were allowed to see our families which would come up to us for about 30 minutes every day. Marta and Milena put up a good front for me, telling me that they were all right. The same did Eva, who had to have all kinds of difficulties these since she was pregnant. In any case our girls held their own! Later Marta told me that right the next day she asked for a bucket, hot water, scrubbing brush and some rags and scrubbed her partition. An older gentleman, Russian, who was in there since 1946(!) came to see her after that. "Madam", he told her, "let me kiss your hand. Since you are the first lady here who scrubbed her partition!" Marta learned from him, that he cannot get anyplace from here, since when he was a young man, and didn't want to join the Bolshevik army in the Soviet Union, he punctured his lung with a knitting needle. After the puncture healed, on an X-ray it looked like a Tuberculosis caused would, and no country wanted to let him in, so he was stuck there.

After those two weeks Franta and I were allowed to join our families. We were all very happy to be all together again. Marta introduced me to the other occupants of our "big room". Unfortunately, I do not remember much about most of them any more. There was a man from Australia, who left Czechoslovakia right after the communists came in 1948, and after spending few years in a refugee camp in Germany, ended up in Australia. After many years his mother in Czechoslovakia had fallen ill, and asked him to come visit her. He was an Australian citizen by then, so he didn't think there was any danger for him to do so. After he got out of the train in Prague (he took the train from Germany where he flew from Australia) a couple of plain-clothes secret agents approached him. A brief conversation followed after which they took his Australian passport and put him to jail for six months. As it happened, he never lost his Czechoslovakian citizenship, so legally they could put him in jail, as he was sentenced to those 6 months in absentia for "illegally" leaving Czechoslovakia for Germany in 1948. As soon as he got out, he spent some time with his mother, who eventually died. After that he found a way to get out of the country again, and was now in Triskirchen waiting for his repatriation back to Australia.

JUST ANOTHER ORDINARY LIFE

We have learned that there is an English language course going to start the next day. Marta, Milena and I together with Eva and Franta have signed up for it right away. There was about twenty of us in the classroom, nobody speaking English and some of us speaking German. Each of us got a picture book with English words beside the pictures. The teacher would pronounce the words and we would try to remember them by writing them in a lined noted book. After an hour of this process, we all left with tremendous head-aches for our room. That would be repeated three times a week. As you can imagine, it was a very slow and tedious process.

During our third week, in Triskirchen, on a very nice and sunny day Milena, Marta and I came to the office by the main gate and asked for permission to visit the town. Our wish was granted and we could leave the compound for two hours. It was actually our first encounter with the free world we so haphazardly chose to live in. I remember how amazed we were with the abundant availability of just about everything we could think of. Our about 100 Shillings didn't go too far, but we were able to buy some oranges, apples, Rama margarine and chocolate for Milena. Fortunately, none of us smoked, so all the pocket money could be spent on extra (for us unusual) fruit and food.

At another time we again asked for a little bit longer permission, and went by a street car to a nearby resort town Baden. We enjoyed the beautiful streets and parks of this very pretty town very much. A cup of coffee and hot chocolate was a perfect finish to a beautiful day.

During the third week in Triskirchen we were all asked to go and get to be registered for a country we would eventually want to live in. As originally agreed, we all registered for Canada, where in the meantime, Pavel and Lid were already settled in. After three months of intensive English language studies Pavel got a job in a newly built dyehouse in Truro, Nova Scotia, near on the other side of Canada. He was Flown there and Lida followed by train across the country. The dye house was not operating yet, so Pavel, already drawing his salary, was there working at anything necessary. After Lida's arrival they got a small apartment to live in and slowly settled down. Marta and I figured that having a brother there might be a plus for us too.

A moth passed by when we were all called into the main office and were told that we would be moved from Triskirchen into a refugee camp especially designed for us. We were getting used to Triskirchen, so every change in our uncertain lives were perceived with caution and mistrust. We said good-byes to our fellow "roommates" who were enviable as they believed that anywhere has got to be better than here.

Well, they were right!

After about two hours van ride due west, often alongside the blue Danube River meandering through spring green valleys, past clean picturesque towns, we arrived to medieval town Grein, not too far from provincial capital Linz, with the Alp mountains visible in the far distance. From Grein it was a short, about a five mile long hop, into the pre-Alp mountain town Bad Kreuzen.

Bad Kreuzen, just like all Austrian towns, was clean as a whistle, sprawled on a green mountainside overlooking a wide valley. The "Fursorgenheim" (Home for people in need), our destination was just 5 minute walk from Bad Kreuzen. It was a white, four large two story high buildings, compound run by the Austrian Government and the UN together. After registering in the main office, we were given keys to a room on the second floor with a large window. Partially obstructed by a pretty spruce tree overlooking the deep ravine. The room was bright, some 9 x 12 feet painted white with two comfortable bunk beds on each side of it. There was also a night stand, a dining table with three chairs, two free standing closets, and mainly a wash basin with running cold and hot water.

Eva and Franta got a similar room, on the first floor, but in a different building.

It was easier to get used to better conditions. Having hot water in the room, two times a week hot showers, rooms cleaned once a week, enclosed bathrooms, situated on the main hall, in perfect condition, three times a day meals served to us in a restaurant style in a spacious dining room with table-cloths and porcelain dishes was just something we didn't dare imagine before. Even a medical doctor and a small hospital were on the premises as well as a room in which priests and pastors of various denominations would hold services once a week.

We felt like being in heaven!

Especially Milena, who, finally, was able to get out, find friends amongst the many kids there, really appreciated our new lifestyle. Our leaving behind everything, all her family and friends, had to be very traumatic for her. Though she wasn't even nine yet, she behaved remarkably well, trying hard not to add any burdens to our difficult situation. Not even running through a closed glass door did not slow her down. Marta and I were very grateful for that as we realized how difficult for a young child this had to be.

Besides many Czechs there were many Slovaks, Yugoslavs, Rumanians, Bulgarians and other European eastern-bloc countries people who were fortunate enough, just like us, to escape their oppressive regimes. Everybody was full of hope, ready to work hard at any job at any of the countries they would eventually end in. I do not remember how many, but I am sure that there were around a couple of hundred families there.

Again, in the Gad Kreuzen school house, English language course was offered which we all attended once a week. I would write down the English words, their pronunciation and meaning in a lined booklet which I constantly carried with me, memorizing spelling every change I got. Marta and I made several friendships with other Czech families there, friendships that lasted for all these years, even when we ended up in different countries, we always stayed in touch. When people are in difficult circumstances, hanging there without knowing what is going to happen to them, somehow, they tend to stick together through the thick and thin. Friendships like that do last for the lifetime. We were all very grateful for all the help we were getting.

Marta, Milena and I would take long strolls in the surrounding woods and mountain meadows full of blooming wild flowers. We were taken care of, but still, in the backs of our minds there was the uncertainty what is going to happen with us? Because of that we really could not enjoy the free time we were all having as well as we could.

Eva and Franta registered for Australia since they wanted their baby born in the place of their future home. Australia took people in the shortest waiting time. When Eva wrote home about their decision, her father, my uncle Pepa got a permission to visit her and Franta after he declared that he wants to go and try to persuade them to come back to Czechoslovakia. He arrived for a two day visit, and was hopeful that they will return with him, especially when Eva's mother wanted them to come back. He left disappointed and alone. So in about a month Eva and Franta were on their way to Australia.

At the end of spring, I and a few other heads of families finally got an invitation to go to Vienna to see someone at the Canadian Embassy about our requests to emigrate to Canada.

The Home van took us there.

I and the others were ushered into a room to fill up a long questionnaire about our professions, abilities, financial situation, contacts in Canada and so on. After filling the questionnaire, we had to wait for a couple of hours for the final decision. When my name was called, I went into an office where man, speaking Czech, told me that, unfortunately, we would not be allowed to go to Canada. The reason for it was that my profession, textile dyer, was not required. After pointing out my brother Pavel already being there, I was told that it does not have any bearing on our situation as he is only establishing himself there, and would not be in any position to help us.

I was completely crushed!

When arriving back to Bad Kreuzen and telling Marta and Milena my sad news we just didn't know what to do. We knew that we could go to Germany, where Marta Marta would get substantial help. This solution did not appeal to us at all. I wrote home about our predicament and got a letter back stating that my mom will contact someone in Great Britain who is in a leading position in a large textile mill and who, possibly, could employ me. Also, she was going to contact a Mr. and Mrs. T. in California (yes, the same whom my father in as about 20 years ago practically saved their lives) who operated a small dye house there. These were very good news.

Without delay we re-registered for the USA. This registration process is a time consuming one. We would again have to go through several interviews and medical screenings. Finally, we got a word that our registration was accepted and is being established to help all refugees (which totaled about 10,000 people) from Czechoslovakia after the Soviet occupation.

We got a very friendly letter from Mr. F from Great Britain, which also included a two year working permit for me. The door to G.B. was thus completely to us! At about the same time we also got a letter from Mrs. T stating that they, too, could employ me as a physical laborer, if I would get all the necessary permits. After talking over the whole situation with Marta we decided that we would rather go to California and be closer to Pavel. "If we have to be poor, let's be poor in the richest country in the world" was our conclusion. In any event our registration for the U.S. was already in process, so that, too weighed in our decision.

While all this was going on a delegation from Sweden arrived, and everybody who wanted to, regardless of his age, medical situation, political inclination, in short anybody was welcomed to go to Sweden right away! Some of our friends took the opportunity and went, spending the rest of their lives happily in Sweden. Later we learned that even the older Russian gentleman from Traiskirchen went to Sweden. We felt very happy for him. The whole action was a great example of the Swedes humanitarian nature.

Some other friends, who registered for the U.S. right from the beginning got a flight date to New York and left. Soon they sent us a letter from some Appalachian Mountain resort where she got a job as a chamber maid in a very posh establishment and he got a job as a grounds keeper there. They were happy as larks! Every letter contained many bitter-humorous situations the new immigrants encountered.

News like that spread through the compound like wildfire. Everybody felt better and was just hoping for an early departure.

During our about seven months stay in Bad Kreuzen we have had several visitors. My father came to see us for two days. He too, got permission under the same notion of trying to talk us into coming back with him. In contrast with uncle Pepa my father did not come to change our minds. He realized that we most likely will not be able to see each other for many years, if ever. It had to be a difficult time for my parents when both of us, Pavel and I suddenly decided to leave for good, but once we landed in Austria, they never tried to change our minds.

Herta with Arnost and their daughter Eva came to visit us for a couple of days. Herta tried to persuade us to go to Germany, but when seeing the possibility of my being employed in my profession in California, she, too realized that it probably would be best for us. Unfortunately, we never saw Herta again. In a couple of years, she died of cancer. We didn't see Eva any more as well. She died tragically in a car accident.

Several friends from Krasna Lipa (after we have sent them invitations as promised before) and Rumburk stopped by to see what how refugee life is all about. After seeing with their own eyes, they also decided to ask for asylum. Some ended up in Sweden, some in Luxemburg. We always kept in touch.

We were not supposed to seek a job there, so we would not take jobs from the locals. Somehow, though, I got a word that a job for me would be available in Grein. It would be great to make some extra money, so I accepted and got a job with a company installing new phone cables. Boy, what a job! This medieval town of Grein had all its streets paved with ancient cobble stones! I guess, since we were paid very little, we would come cheaper to the company than using heavy digging machinery. So, a bunch of us, emigrants, would be digging out those cobble stones and dig trenches using just picks and shovels. I never worked so hard in my life! The job lasted about three weeks, and I was glad when there was an end to it. Another job landed, just for a couple of days, was as extra in in filming some half-porn film "Black Cat" taking place in some medieval times. I was just part of the crowd, dressed in cloths from those times, milling in the town square, talking with other similarly dressed men and women. Those were easy earned money.

Finally in September we got a word that our transport will be leaving on September 26th from Vienna to New York, where a representative of our sponsor (everybody coming to the U.S. had to have a sponsor) AFCR will meet us and direct us wherever will be needed.

So, after many teary good-byes with our friends and thanks to the Fursorgenheim representatives we all got in the van and were taken to the Vienna airport. Received our flight tickets and boarded a special airplane full of our co-refugees bound for New York.

Miroslav Kolias

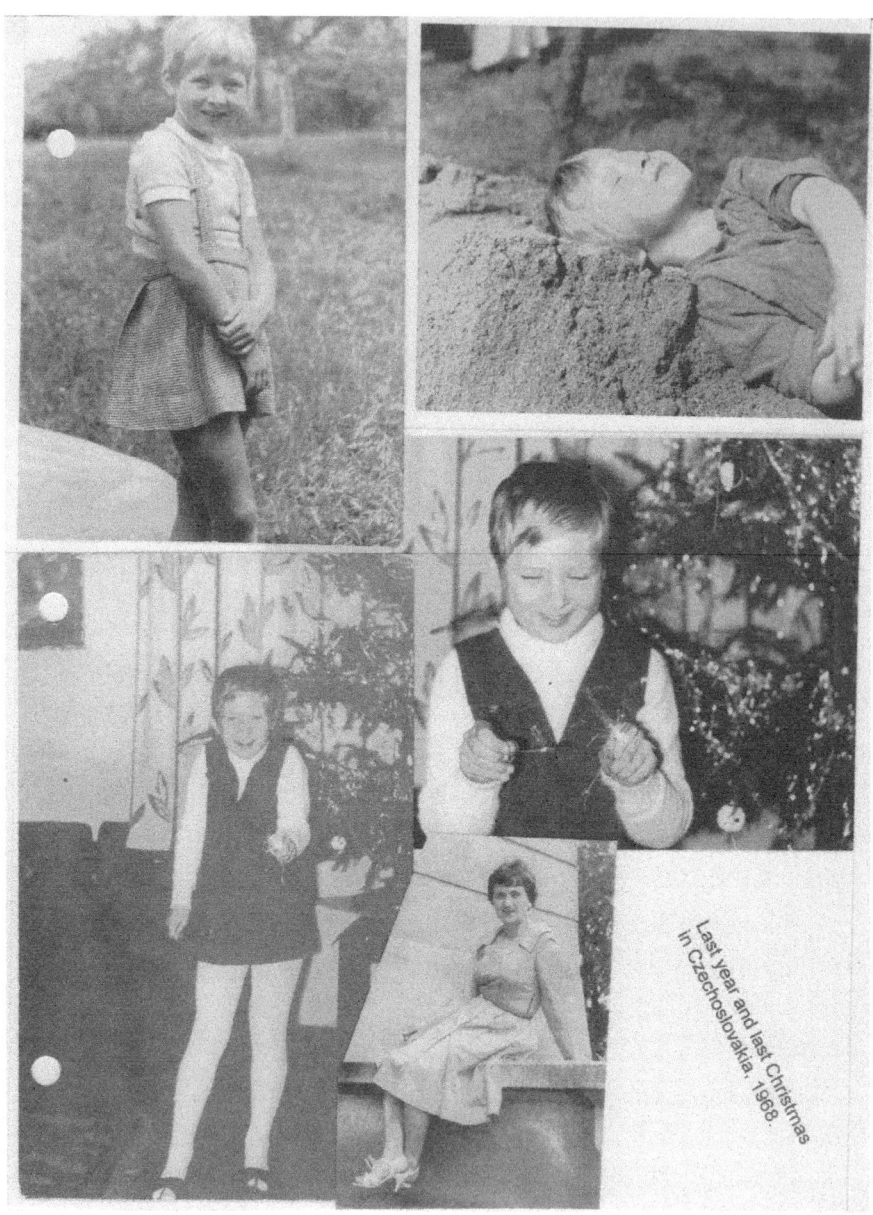

Last year and last Christmas in Czechoslovakia. 1968.

JUST ANOTHER ORDINARY LIFE

Clockwise from the top:

We could not enjoy fully our six months "vacation" in Bad Kreuzen. Uncle Pepa could not persuade Eva to return home with him. My father was OK with our decision to leave.
It was hard for him to say good-bye. Are we going to see each other again? Herta, Arnost and Rudi also came to wish us good luck.
Little money for acting as the "crowd" came handy.

The fourth beginning.

I'll never forget the night view of New York after the long and uneventful flight across Atlantic. Just before approaching the America's shore our flight attendants walked through the whole plane and sprayed a fresh flower scent all over us. We thought that they just wanted to welcome us to freedom with this friendly gesture. Only many days later we realized that the flower scent was to suppress our body odors that permeated all our clothes and belongings, regardless at what country we originated in. There was about 200 of us coming from all parts of Eastern Europe dominated by Soviet Union. There were people from Bulgaria, Romania, Poland, Hungary and other states, and of course Czechoslovakia which group amounted to most of us. In Europe people are not so sensitive to body odor like their counterparts in the U.S. are. But, since we decided to live there, we would have to assimilate and take American customs (no doubt better in this case) as our own.

Let's come back to our first New York view, though. The airplane got ready to prepare for landing and was cruising over a sea of bright lights, the brightest ones, shining over a green grass, being on some unusually shaped sport field which the more knowledgeable of us identified as a baseball field. I never saw anything like it in my life! It stayed permanently etched in my brain.

Our excitement peaked at the successful landing for which we awarded our pilot with thunderous applause.

OK, so here we are!

What is going to happen with my family and me in this completely unknown to us country? Are we going to succeed against all odds, or are we going to fail miserably?

These and other questions kept running through our minds as we gathered our meager belongings carefully fitted in two small suitcases carried with us on board. It seemed forever to get off the plane and into a bus that took us all into a cavernous hall. Customs check and issuing Alien Numbers that became our representation for the next few years followed like in a dream. After that, representatives of different sponsor organizations, carrying large identification boards, greeted us.

For the AFCR there was Mr. Jerabek with a list of his "souls". As he would read the individual names, he would also tell them where are they going to go. There were some who stayed in New York, but others would be directed to Pittsburgh, Dallas, Miami etc. forming small groups, waiting for further directives as where to go for the next part of their trip to vast unknown. When our name was read, I showed Mr. Jerabek the letter from Mr. T. as a promise of an employment for me in Union City, California. After explaining that Union City is close-by to San Francisco, Mr. Jerabek arranged for three tickets there via Chicago, adding the expense to our bill for transportation from Austria to the U.S. that swelled by it to $ 950.- As per agreement with AFCR we were to pay-off our first American debt within a year time after landing my first job here. Mr. Jerabek called a taxi that took us to a different airport, discharging us in front of the needed airline for our trip to Chicago.

I really do not remember how we managed to find our plane, get on it and get off in Chicago. Once there a friendly attendant pointed us all to the next counter for our connecting flight to San Francisco.

We had some time to wait, so I decided that I have to call Mr. T. and let him know about our arrival. I did have his number, but had no idea how to dial it. After lifting a public phone receiver, I was greeted with a completely non-understandable language, so I decided to ask an attendant for help and went to find one. Without telling Marta and Milena where I was going I found an attendant around the corner and after difficult explanation she dialed the number for me .Freshly awakened Mr. T. in California (it was only 2 AM there!) was glad to hear from us and promised to pick us up at the S.F. airport after our arrival. Returning back to Marta and Milena I was greeted with almost tears as they did not know where did I go?

"Well", it was my Czech reply "I am sorry, but I had to think in English and I was not able to do so with you around". Marta never forgot that and many times brought that up when talking to our friends about our comings here....

Mr. and Mrs. T. picked us up on the San Francisco Airport in early morning of Saturday, September 27th 1969 (coincidentally the date being our 11th wedding anniversary) and drove us across (at that time) the longest bridge on Earth spanning the San Francisco Bay. Our first night in California we were to spend in the San Leandro Nimitz motel where they booked a room for us. They left to let us catch up with our sleep and a promise that they will pick us up in the afternoon.

We just realized that we did not sleep for some 40 hours. After shower we got in our beds and slept till about two o'clock. We ate something we brought with us from Austria and went out to explore. Naturally I wanted to lock our room behind us, so I inserted the key and turned it. Just to be sure I checked the door and to my astonishment it was still open! I tried again, this time turning the key in the other direction, tried the door - it was still open! After several tries, I gave up and went for a help which I found in a lady who was cleaning the next room. After some difficult (we did not know English) explanation she finally understood what I was trying to tell her. With a smile she opened our room door, turned the little thing in the middle of the door knob on the inside, stepped out, made sure that I still have my key, closed the door and tried it. My gosh, it was locked!

That was our introduction to a spring-loaded door lock. Similar experiences we would have many in the coming days.

It was a bright and unusually for us warm late September day when we first stepped out on California soil on our own. Tall palm trees and bright flowers of all kinds greeted us. The street was very different from a street in a European city. Wooden houses, wide streets full of large cars, nobody on the sidewalks. Completely unfamiliar sight.

Are we going to get used to all this? Well, we will have to!

We did not want to miss Mrs. T. so after about twenty minutes we returned back to our room. She arrived as promised and took us to their dye house in Union City where I was to be employed. The dye house was entirely different from what I was accustomed, too. Different machinery, different chemicals and dye names, different procedures.

Mr. T. showed me around explaining the machinery and procedures. I realized that everything will be OK once I learn a little more about it. I was also introduced to Mr. Joe Franco, owner of the neighboring carpet mill for which Mr. T. dyed woolen yarns to make custom carpets from. While this was going on Mrs. T. drove Marta and Milena to a Hayward motel off Mission Boulevard near downtown for the night and bought them food. Originally, we were supposed to be staying in a close-by apartment, but it was not available yet. In the meantime, I was to stay in a small motel in Union City for $ 2.- a night, close to the dye house so I could walk to work. In that motel ladies would not be permitted to stay as there was only one bathroom to a floor. As this was a Saturday, I was to start the next Monday for a $ 1.65/hr a minimum wage at that time. That was just fine with me.

I stayed a little longer in the dye house observing procedures and when Mrs. T. returned, she took me to my motel at the corner of Union City Blvd. and Smith Street. I got a small room with a bed, night stand and a closet, and was happy to hit the sack as soon as possible. I slept as a baby. Around 10 o'clock on the Sunday morning Mrs. T came and took me to Marta's motel. There we learned that Marta and Milena hardly slept at all, as the motel was used primarily by prostitutes and their Johns for short stays. Mrs. T. did some phoning and then took us all to a nice motel in San Leandro, just off 580 freeway. It was a very nice place, with a large room, a small kitchenet and private bath. The proprietor lent her iron to Marta to iron our clothes that, so far, were still in our suitcases. The price per night was $ 11.- that we gladly paid having $ 125.- in our possession. Since I was given a job right away, we could live on that! After settling down we went to a nearby small grocery store and bought some staples to sustain Marta and Milena in this motel and me in the Union City one. Toward the evening Mrs. T. came to pick me up again and deliver me to my motel. I wouldn't see or talk to Marta and Milena for a whole week.

Monday by eight o'clock in the morning, right at the work starting hour, I reported for duty to Mr. T. and was assigned to Tony and Miguel, the two employees Mr. T. was employing full time. Besides them there were also few students over 16 years old employed part time. Their work experience was counted as a grade toward their graduation. Everybody, save for Mr. and Mrs. T., knew about as much Czech as I did Spanish or English. Fortunately, we got along fine and they all tried hard to introduce me into what was happening in the dye house. I had to learn how to load yarn into machines, how to operate them, how to operate steam producing boilers, how to make additions of dyes and chemicals into machines etc. Everything was entirely different to what I was accustomed to. Especially I was surprised by the way steam was generated. Back home steam generating was a large part of textile dyeing business, involving many people and equipment to haul tons of coal for the large boilers that had to be fired some 4 hours before dye house starting time to generate enough steam pressure to be used in dye machines. Here, there were three small natural gas fired boilers, that required in the morning just to push a button and within 15 minutes there was steam ready for usage! What a difference in productivity! I worked in the dye house for the whole day every day, even so I was paid for 8 hour shifts only, just to get familiar with the place. I didn't have anything else to do in my motel anyway.

After the next Saturday shift was over Mrs. T. took me to Marta's motel. We were very happy to be all together again and went out for a walk in our neighborhood. We marveled over the nice houses with flowering yards and wondered if we, too, one day will be able to live in one just like these. In a small grocery store we bought our first candy bar and shared it between the three of us. To our surprise, beside all the sweet ingredients it also contained salt which we did not like. Gradually, though, we got used to the taste and nowadays we do not even notice the presence of salt in them.

On Sunday Mrs. T. came to pick us up and took us to the Gemco store to get some needed things as by the next week we should have our apartment ready. Our first trip to a supermarket was, again, overwhelming to us. We never saw anything like it. Rows and rows of merchandise of all kinds, the sheer abundance of everything was unbelievable. It reminded us slightly of our trip to Germany, but just more so of everything. We bought all kinds of things, including dishes and such for our future apartment. Few pieces of those dishes we actually still have today as a remembrance to our first days here.

In the middle of the week our apartment was ready to move in.

Well, it was supposed to be ready.

The apartment was a part of four small double unit houses that at one time served as soldier barracks, now remade to small one bedroom apartments. There was a small living room, a tiny bedroom, a tiny kitchen, a toilet and shower. We appreciated, though, that even this small, very neglected and uninviting apartment had a running hot water.

There were no curtains or any other window coverings and there was no furniture either. To have some privacy at night, we unrolled a large linoleum roll, standing in the corner of the living room to cover the windows. Mrs. T. lent us her camping cooking dishes, two blankets and a cot for Milena to sleep on. She also arranged for the PG&E services for which we had to borrow $ 35.- interest free from her, because we had to pay $ 75.- for the first month rent that took all of our money. Luckily, we did not have to pay the last month rent right away. I paid our second American debt off in the next seven weeks by Mr. T. subtracting $ 5.- each week from my pay check.

By now I was familiar with all the manual work in the dye house so Mr. T. let me work 12 hours (paid this time) a day, from noon till the midnight. I appreciated that as it meant a little bit more money for us. After about six months there I was also getting a five cents an hour raise every week from then on.

Milena was surprisingly resilient to all of these changes in our life. She took them as they came, without any resentment or complaints. As soon as we moved into the Horner Street apartment, Milena enrolled into the local Alvarado elementary school. By her age she was supposed to go into the third grade, but since she didn't know English, she was enrolled into the second grade.

At the end of that grade, she did so well that the next school year she was enrolled into the fourth grade, thus catching up the lost year. I remember that on one of the first days we moved into the apartment, she was outside playing with a neighbor's cat. Suddenly the cat got spooked of a stray dog and it took off Milena's embrace scratching and bloodying Milena's face with its claws. Poor Marta had to deal with that by just using water and towel to stop the bleeding. Next day Milena had to go to school with her face all scratched up. Coming back home she sported nice Band-Aids over her wounds.

That evening Milena's teacher, Mrs. Hedden, came to see Marta and Milena, we guessed just to see what kind of people Milena's parents are that they let her go to school without dressing her wounds. Mrs. Hedden invited Marta and Milena out to eat and with the help of a dictionary they were able to understand each other. When Marta mentioned to Mrs. Hedden that we are not going to stay for long in this apartment, she just looked at Marta in a way that communicated to Marta as Mrs. Hedden thinking: "Well, when someone is living like you are, he is not moving anywhere". Mrs. Hedden visit brought us a break, though, as Milena's school lent us for every week-end a special language learning machine. It consisted of spoken English words which we would listen to, and after that would speak the same word back into the machine which, in turn, would play it back to us, so we could hear the difference between the correct and our pronunciation. Today Milena speaks without any trace of Czech accent while Marta and I still have some of it. I guess, when you are a child, you learn much quicker and better than an adult.

We did not have any furniture in the apartment. By the road, in front of the apartments, there was a discarded couch laying to be picked-up by anyone. We took it in. It was very dirty, but after a thorough cleaning, it was usable. To make it even better we kept saving the plastic bread wrappings, cut them open, lay them over the couch fabric and cover the whole assembly by a sheet to sleep on.

One day two nice wooden chairs, upholstered with cowboy theme fabric, appeared in front of our door together with a bag of small used soap bars. Eventually we learned and met Charlie and Clara, a Canadian and an English lady, who managed a small motel in Oakland. Charlie also worked as a wood man with one of our neighbors. After learning about us, having nothing, he brought those two chairs and soap bars to us. We became very good friends for many, many years.

Save for one pair that was a white lady and a black man, all the other families in our apartments were of Mexican origin. We could not wish for better neighbors. When Marta did first clothes washing (in her hands, of course), she wanted to hang the clothes to dry on a line strung outside between two trees. It was a windy day, and as Marta was trying to somehow keep the clothes on the line, suddenly one of the neighbor ladies appeared with a bunch of cloth pins. At another time the black-and-white couple brought us a small kitchen table. The man who worked with Charlie brought us used, but still working TV set that he wanted to discard. We could not understand what was said on the programs, but gradually we got the "music" of the American English in our ears which helped us a lot down the road. On one of the first days a box full of cans with various foods, drinks and fresh vegetables was brought to us by our neighbors. It was the first time we tasted Root-beer, another unfamiliar taste to us. We were overwhelmed by our neighbors' kindness (especially when we realized that they, too, were of rather meager means) and were sorry that we couldn't even properly thank them for it.

Yes, such were the first days of our new lives. Interestingly, we never think of them in bad terms. These experiences were to stay with us for the rest of our lives.

And they were happy experiences!

Horner Street, Union City.

The Horner Street marched straight due west toward the San Francisco Bay. It dead-ended by a fence dividing the inhabitable part of Union City from marshy plains surrounding the Bay. This part of Union City had the best climate, as there was just about constant breeze coming from the sea, cooling the air in summer hot days and warming the cold ones in winter. Behind our apartment, toward the Bay, there was just one more house, a two story dwelling at the end of the street. This house used to be occupied by several young men, most likely undocumented workers from Mexico. They kept to themselves, renting rooms, three to four of them to a room.

Our apartment was the second one coming on the dirt alley from the street. Our units were set some 10 feet back from the street and in the so formed empty space there were two metal barrels used to burn garbage in. Constant crown of light smoke and smell lingered over them. There were also mail boxes, identified by the apartment numbers, each fastened to some 3 feet tall wooden beam. Two steps led to a 3 feet square covered entrance to our main door. Milena would keep a small dish full of Friskies for the neighborhood cats there.

Since I was working the noon to midnight shift and Milena would go to school, in her "free" time Marta would be home trying to improve our apartment by constant scrubbing and cleaning. To Marta's horror there seemed to be no end of roaches coming from under the old refrigerator and stove at night time. Milena's school bus stopped about 100 yards from our apartments. Marta would accompany Milena to the bus in the morning and pick her up in the afternoon. On Sundays we would walk to the Union City Blvd. down the road and take care of shopping for the next week. There was a small corner store carrying liquor and most of the food items we needed. There was also a small butcher shop, ran by a Chinese man, where we would mostly buy ham and chicken, two very expensive (and hard to get) items back home. Here those two items were the cheapest ones to get. We would joke about it, saying that at least the food is good and plentiful. While Marta was shopping in the butcher store, I would stay outside as I could not stand the stench in there. I guess the fact that the store floor was covered by old sawdust contributed to the smell.

We knew that in order to better our position we have to save as much as we could. Marta, always an excellent home maker, saw to it. Milena was very cooperative, too. I do not remember Milena asking for anything special just for her.

Marta kept a list of all the expenses. I remember one such entrance in her list. She bought two small lady bug pins to hold Milena's hair. The price: 25 Cents. To justify her "splurging" Marta added to the item: "But they are very nice!" Every time we came across this in the later years, we had a hearty laugh about it.

Every day I would walk to work for about one and a half miles. After about a week suddenly a car came alongside me and stopped. From it an elderly, tall gentleman alighted and asked me if I was selling anything. He explained to me that he keeps seeing me coming down the street at the same time every day and was curious who I was, as I was the only person walking the street. In my broken English I tried to explain to him our situation. He introduced himself as Joseph Silva, recently retired and living in the third house down the street from our apartment. He offered to take me to work, which I gladly accepted. Since then, we kept in touch with Mr. Silva (as we always called him), his wife Mrs. Mae Silva and son Kenneth who, being of my age, was for his entire life confined to a wheel chair. His birth was a very difficult one. The Doctor had to use a special tool to help Ken into this world and by doing so he damaged Ken's head to a degree that Ken could not speak nor to take care of himself. Because of that Mrs. Silva had to stay at home all the time taking care of her son. The Silva's didn't have any friends as it was difficult for them to socialize in their small house with Ken being there. We, on the other hand, were happy to acquire life-long friends who took time and pain to communicate with us in English.

For the first Thanksgiving in California, we were invited to Mr. and Mrs. T. and had a very nice time with them. Thanksgiving is one of the most important holidays in the States.

The next day we were invited to Charlie and Clara to continue the celebration. Clara cooked a typical meal with yams, roasted turkey, cranberry and pumpkin pie. All three of us enjoyed the evening very much. Armed with a dictionary on our part and a good will on our hosts part we were actually able to carry a conversation. Charlie told us about difficulties they encountered managing the motel. They were robbed several times, so Charlie put a two-way mirror in the door leading to the motel office. While Clara would be helping customers in the office, Charlie would be standing on the other side of the door and look in through the mirror, a gun in his hand. As it happened a customer, Clara was attending to, pulled out a gun and asked for all the money in the register. Seeing that Charlie did not wait any longer and pulled the trigger, shooting the man through the mirror wounding him. The man fled, but was apprehended later by police. To our friend's astonishment, the guy, while in jail, brought a case against Charlie stating that the shooting was a much stronger response to his only asking for money! Charlie had a very difficult time and an expense hiring a lawyer to have the case against him dismissed. "Boy, what a country!" we mused. How could it be that one is being robbed, is defending himself and at the end is being prosecuted? What a nerve the robber had!

After three months we managed to save about $ 500.- and decided to contact Marta's cousin Draha Michalek in Lafayette. We did not want to impose on them until we would be somewhat established here.

The following Sunday Draha with his wife Zdena showed up at our door! They greeted us very warmly and could not believe in what condition the place we lived in was. Marta didn't see Draha since they both were very young, so talking and more talking just wouldn't stop.

Draha emigrated right in 1948 after the Communist took over in Czechoslovakia to Germany. Once there he met Zdena and married her there. They had to wait for couple of years to get from Germany to Australia so Tony, their first child, son Tony was born in Germany. Once in Australia, after a month-long ship voyage there, Draha worked as a truckdriver delivering vegetables and fruit from the fields to stores. Zdena tended to Tony, living out in the boonies in a tiny apartment with corrugated metal walls and roof, hot in summer, cold in winter. Their daughter Eva was born there. As soon as they put together enough money for Draha's ticket to California he came here, got employed in a car repair shop, and after he put together enough money, brought Zdena and the kids to himself. Eventually he started his own car repair shop in Berkeley and they bought a nice house in Lafayette.

Right the next Saturday Draha came back armed with paint and roller, and while I was working, he managed to paint our apartment. He also brought and installed a portable electric heater and a small metal book-shelf. They also gave us very warm two sleeping bags. Boy, what a difference to come home into a clean and warm apartment! Things started to look much "brighter" for us.

Mr. and Mrs. T. offered to take us all to "Sokol" for the New Year's Eve. "Sokol" is a very old Czech sport organization specializing in calisthenics and other sports. A chapter of "Sokol" was established in San Francisco many years ago when the Czech population steadily grew there. Nowadays, an estimate of some 4,000 or more Czech families live in California. Marta was worried that, since it was a night event, there wouldn't be any kids for Milena to talk to. We were assured that there would be plenty of kids there and that we would have an opportunity to meet other Czech families, so we gratefully accepted the invitation.

As it turned out, though, there weren't any other children Milena's age, so after a good dinner most of the gathered people started to drink and dance to a Czech band music. Marta and I felt rather uncomfortably to mingle leaving Milena sitting by the table all alone, so we didn't, and were just watching what was going on around us. We did meet some other Czech people, but none of them remained as our friends in the future. Around midnight Milena started to cry and wished to go home. Since we were dependent on the Mr. and Mrs. T. transportation, we didn't get out of there until some 2 o'clock in the morning. As far as I remember we visited the "Sokol" hall only once after that in all the rest of almost forty years of living here.

Draha and Zdena took us on several occasions in their large Ford to show us around California. Almost every Sunday they would come and take us out to the Sierra foothills, Mont Diablo, the Delta and so on. We were very grateful for this.

Miroslav Kolias

One other Sunday Miguel, one of the fulltime employees of the Dye House, came and took us to San Francisco. We could barely communicate with him as he showed us the beach with its carnival-like atmosphere and all the attractions there. We were amazed seeing some grown up people to go into water in their dresses and pants, not minding getting all wet. The hippie movement in San Francisco was well and strong then, but we didn't know anything about it. The coldness of the Pacific surprised us, we thought the ocean would be warm and pleasant to dive in. I guess, what you see in the movies is not necessarily true!

Suddenly our first Christmas in California was approaching. We tried to make it as nice as possible for Milena, which was not an easy task under the circumstances. She was doing remarkably well at school and we wanted somehow to reward her for that, and for her, all around excellent behavior. On the TV they were showing an advertisement for all kinds of toys, and Milena's heart was captured by this about 15" tall dancing ballerina called Dancerina. The doll had a ballerina dress, was standing on her toe, wore a crown and was able to turn around just like a real ballerina. The $ 35.- price was a little bit steep for us, but we decided that she should get the fairy Dancerina. Marta wrapped the box festively and placed it under the small tree we trimmed for Milena as nicely as we could.

Milena's eyes were bright and glowing when she unwrapped the box and saw the Dancerina she wanted so much! When Milena tried Dancerina to dance, she realized that she would have to hold the doll by her crown in order to turn. That was a huge disappointment to Milena as she thought that the doll will be dancing all by herself. In that TV add the hand holding the doll's crown while dancing was not visible. Our hearts ached for Milena and her disappointment. As much as Milena wanted that doll, she very seldom would play with it and finally completely abandoned it. Well, we realized that the advertising is not always what it seems to be.

Mr. and Mrs. T. invited us for Christmas to their place in Hayward. We welcomed that very much and have spent a very nice day with them, so the Christmas was not a total disaster. Milena actually perked-up and was happy to play with Vera and Helenka. Milena got very nice clothes from Mr. and Mrs. T. which we appreciated very much.

By this time we could speak English sparingly, but in such a way that we could actually communicate, albeit very primitively. One day Marta, on her way from her part-time job at Colonial Carpet Mill, went to the local corner grocery store to get some things. As she was selecting her shopping, she realized that there was some dispute going on between the store owner and two customers by the store register. Marta was approaching the register with her shopping to pay for it when, suddenly, the store owner took an open catchup bottle from the counter and threw it at one of the two men. That guy ducked and the ketchup splattered all over the front of Marta's new coat! Those two guys disappeared quickly and the store owner tried to console crying Marta who was still not able to communicate her frustrations to him. Luckily Marta was able to clean her coat up in the store restroom.

As we did not have a car, we had to rely on the local small stores that, invariably, were more expensive than far away supermarkets. So, we decided that it's time to try and get a car for ourselves. Marta called Draha (we had a phone by that time!) and asked him if he could locate some small car for us. Sure enough, by the end of January 1970 Draha told us that he's got a 1964, 6 cylinder Dodge Dart with slanted engine available from one of his customers. The price $ 425.- was right up our alley, so we happily asked him to secure it for us.

Next Sunday Draha came to get us and took us to Lafayette to pick-up our first car in our lives. It was a white two door sporty looking car with red upholstery and automatic transmission, but with no power steering nor power brakes! I loved it at the first sight!

Driving it was another matter completely. Draha showed me what and how, and I tried it, actually pretty successfully for the first time after a very long time since my last driving back home. I decided that I was brave (and foolish) enough to bring my first car home by myself. Draha, driving in front of me, was slowly guiding me through Lafayette and in the freeway slow lane all the way home, where I arrived completely drenched in sweat.

VOW! We have our own car!

Between our apartments there was just enough space to park two cars there. Mr. Silva was delighted to see that we have a transportation on our own, and offered to teach me more about driving, parking and basic maintenance. I was an eager student, and since then I love to drive.

It was customary for us, even when our income was a very meager one, to be sending some money back home to our families. When we announced that we have a car (something only very few people at that time at home had) they thought that we are sitting on a pile of gold. It was very difficult to explain our true situation by mail to them, since they did not have phones at home.

At the beginning of summer, we tried to get better living conditions for us. By this time Marta was working at Colonial Carpet Mills in their sample department making carpet samples for sale reps. She was working on a sewing machine, even so that, before we left home, she said that she will do anything, but sewing once we are abroad. The extra money she made we always saved and so were able to better our position.

JUST ANOTHER ORDINARY LIFE

Clockwise from the top:
First apartment on Homer Street in Union City, CA, 1969.
With Dancerina, Christmas 1969.
Milena is starting to grow hair, 1969.
Thanksgiving at Mr. & Mrs. Teyrovsky, 1969.
With Mrs. Silva and son Ken, 1968.
At Draha and Zdena Michalek, 1969.
With our first car Dodge Dart, 1970.
Trying to keep it clean, 1970.

Miroslav Kolias

Clockwise from the top:
New apartment at Sleepy Hollow, Hayward. Christmas 1970.
Looks like home, doesn't it?
Marta's Christmas dinner and cookies.
Milena in her new robe putting on her first watch.
Milena is happy with her own furniture, 1971.
Botanical gardens in Berkeley, 1971.
Michalek's came for a visit, 1971.

To Sleepy Hollow.

One of Marta's coworkers lived in an apartment complex on Sleepy Hollow Ave. in Hayward, and told Marta that there is an empty apartment available. Milena just finished her second grade with very good results and was promoted directly to the fourth grade for the next school year, so it was a perfect time for moving.

I went to the office of Lord Tennyson Apartments on Sleepy Hollow in Hayward, situated just across Kaiser Hospital. The lady there explained to me how the complex worked. The apartments were available for low-income families, subsidized by the government. It turned out that we would qualify for the empty apartment. After explaining our situation to her, she promised that she would try and get that empty apartment for us.

The fact that Marta's friend lived there for many years and she gave us very good references helped a lot and so we did get the apartment!

So, in middle of July we thanked Mr. Franco for letting us live in one of his apartments, packed our belongings, and leaving all the furniture behind, moved to the Sleepy Hollow. The large complex consisted of free-standing buildings containing two and four apartment each. Our place was in one of the two apartment buildings, the one on the top. When we saw it the first time, it was just like looking into heaven! The apartment had a large living room with a wall-wide "French" window overlooking landscaped space between two buildings. There also was a small, full electric kitchen, a small hallway leading to a nice bathroom with a tub and shower, the master bedroom and another bedroom. In both bedrooms were built-in closets, and there was a new carpeting throughout the whole apartment!

Even though the apartments were subsidized, the price of $ 141.- a month was double of what we were paying so far. Still, it was worth every Cent of it and we felt very happy to be able to live there. There were pretty strict rules in the complex. No loud music after 10 PM, and if we would have a guest staying more than one night, we would have to let the management know. The common laundry room was in a near-by building, and there was also a club house that could be rented out for larger parties. The whole complex was nicely landscaped, the grass mowed regularly, buildings had a fresh paint on them and the whole impression was a very nice and neat indeed.

The apartment was not furnished. We only had that small metal book-shelf and the TV set, so we had to furnish first Milena's room and get at least a dining table with chairs. At Levitz furniture store in San Leandro we have found a nice, bright yellow girl's bedroom with a twin bed, night stand, dresser, small book-case and a desk. Milena loved it when it was installed the next day, and we were very happy for her. The next Sunday we all went to the Michalek's who took us to Berkeley and into a Danish style furniture store on San Pablo Ave. We liked a changeable blond, European looking dining table and four seat-upholstered chairs. After paying cash, the store delivered everything the next day.

JUST ANOTHER ORDINARY LIFE

Our lives were slowly getting better! From my next pay-check we bought a sofa on sale at J.C. Penney. It was a blue, upholstered item that had at each side two small side-tables attached, very convenient for placing a vase with flowers and magazines on them. After a couple of weeks, we also bought a queen-size bed and mattress for the master bedroom. To our astonishment we were given all the beddings and pillows with it for free!

All this time I was working my 12 hour shifts from noon till midnight, and Marta would work part-time in the morning. I would take Marta to work at 8 AM and pick her up at 11 AM to bring her back home. Milena made some friends with girls from the complex, but mostly would stay home, bettering her English, helping Marta preparing lunch and talking to me before bringing Marta home. Our lives started to get a feeling of normalcy and family living.

It happened that I did not need to work one Saturday, so we decided to take an overnight trip to Yosemite. We knew about Yosemite still from back home after reading about it in several magazines and seeing pictures of Half Dome and El Capitan. The actual sights of them overwhelmed us, though. Our simple Dart delivered us safely past steep, curvy roads and deep valleys on which, at one time I spotted black animals and shouted: "Bears! Look, bears!" only to be laughed at after it was clear that they were not bears, but just black cows. Marta sometimes remembers the incident, and needles me about it until now. Finally, we arrived through beautiful scenery into the Yosemite Valley and the Curry Village where we rented a small, one room cabin with wood stove, two beds and common showers near-by. The whole afternoon we explored Yosemite and marveled over it. Milena even tried her new bathing suit in the river, but would not stay in the water for too long, being so cold from the still melting snows high up in the mountains. The night in the cabin was a nice one, too. The gentle crackling of flames put us all to sleep pretty fast. If we would have known that Milena took with her a jar of honey, opened it and placed it outside of our cabin (for the bears, as she explained to us later), we probably would not sleep that well. Luckily no bears appeared and our lives were saved.

The next morning, we did some more exploring, rented a mule for Milena to ride on, got to the Mirror Lake, Nevada Falls, Bridal Vail Falls and Yosemite Falls, all like being in a kaleidoscope of beauty. Reluctantly we had to leave and head back home. As a souvenir we bought a small, Indian made good spirit statuette with a colored feather on its head. We still have it, and judging by almost 40 years of our good living here, he did a great job for us....

Since I was working very hard, Mr. T. gave me a week of paid vacation before a full year of my work for him as it was originally agreed on. Just about every Sunday we would take a discovery trip into our near or far surroundings. Both, Marta and I loved those trips, and Milena would tag along even though she would be sometimes bored to death. Anyway, we all agreed that it would be nice to take a week-long trip to Oregon, so in August we set for our first trip beyond California borders. It was a very nice trip, even so that we had to stay in inexpensive motels and eat from our cool box most of the time to save money. We took the 101 north, along the water, all the way to Astoria and Columbia River. We visited Portland and Eugene on our way back on the Interstate 5. We loved every minute of it, and often fondly remember it until now. When you think of it, one really does not have to spend a lot of money to see this beautiful and so interesting country. Well, admittedly, we still love to travel, but are doing it in a little bit different "style". Those first trips in the Dart without air-conditioning, power steering and power windows are forever lovingly imbedded in our memories. In all these hectic times we always found time to keep in touch with our friends, like the Silva's, and tried to make new ones. Marta was and still is especially good in this task, her natural ease in approaching people being a great help. I am more of the reclusive type, but glad to be around people once I have known them.

The year was 1970, and Milena started her 4th grade in a new school, (practically fluent in English by now) where she made many new friends, and was happily adapting into her new life. Marta and I were very happy for her, because we realized that by us placing her here, into such a new and different environment, we unknowingly put a huge burden on her young and tender shoulders. It was hard for her to bring her friends home to meet her parents who did not speak well English and whose views on life were still very much affected by their suppressing existence in a Communist regime. Our hearts ached for Milena when in stores she would walk few steps in front of us so people would not associate her with those two strangely speaking people. We knew that Milena loved us very much and that this situation was very hard on her. Luckily, with time (and our improvements) all those first difficulties were forgotten and we are enjoying a very good relationship with Milena and the whole of her new family.

Slowly our second Christmas in California was approaching. It was a much happier and shinier than the first one. One day someone from Macy's called and asked if we would like to get their credit card. "Sure", I said, "but nobody wants to give us one since we have been here only for a short period of time". "Well, you will get one from us" was the answer. And sure enough, our first credit card arrived shortly after that. To establish our credit, we decided to go and to buy something at Macy's using their credit card. So, Marta got her new beige, woolen overcoat, a real beauty for Christmas. Milena, too got different clothes and books. We got again together with the Michaleks and other friends to celebrate.

As a special gift to Milena, we decided to go to Disneyland over the New Year vacations. What a marvelous time we had there! Both, Marta and I, enjoyed Disneyland as much as Milena did. We never saw anything like that and were loving every minute of our time. The nightly Electrical Parade just about took our breath away. The talking Mr. Lincoln statue and all the other wonderful exhibits will stay in our memories forever. We decided that we have to repeat this trip as soon as possible.

We could do that in couple of years and to have some company for Milena we took Arlene and Maricella, Mr. Franco's daughters with us. It was a great trip, the girls got along just fine and everybody was having a very good time. We also visited the Queen Mary in Long Beach. All and all those were very nice days for all of us. Both, Arlene and Maricella as well as the other five brothers and sisters of theirs remained our friends until today.

The last (?) beginning.

Ever since we arrived Mr. and Mrs. T. as well as the Michaleks kept telling us that our first goal should be to buy our own house. Fortunately, we listened to them and geared our lives to that achievement.

Saving moneis for the down payment was our first priority. We tried to live on my wages and Marta's income was put into savings. Because we did that religiously, in the middle of 1971 we have saved enough to be able to start looking for a house.

Close to our apartments we have found a nice three bedroom house with a pretty large living room and a fireplace standing in the middle of it. The house was close to Milena's school, so we thought that it would suit us just fine. We let Michaleks know about our thinking, so the next week-end they came to go with us and take a look at our prospect.

After coming out of the house we asked them, how they liked it?

"Well, it's not bad, but there are several things against it" was the reply, and they started explaining them to us. It turned out that they did not like the location being very close to the school, as there will be always a lot of traffic getting by. The house had a flat roof which was not practical as it was difficult to insulate and thus spending more on heating in winter and cooling in summer. The last objection was that it stood on a flat land prone to flooding.

We would have never thing about all these things! Disappointed, but glad to learn a valuable lesson, we decided to save a little bit more to afford a better situated house. Just about at that time I heard that there are special mortgages available for minorities featuring lower interest rates. Well, I thought to myself, we are minority also, after all how many Czech people are around here? I decided to pursue this lead.

At the AAA office (we became members as soon as we got our Dodge) I got an Oakland map and asked where the county offices handling those special mortgages were located. Next day at 8:30 in the morning I set for Oakland, found that office and went in asking about the minority mortgage loan. Well, they were looking at me like I was a joker! After figuring out that I was not here to make fun of them they explained to me what the term "minority" means. OK, just another lection to a growing set of rules for someone finding his way in a strange country.....

Disappointed, but not discouraged, in next days I kept driving around the town, looking for our dream house, until someone told me that I should go and see a real estate agent, that it does not cost anything to ask and to be shown several houses in our price range. With Marta we decided that we would try to get a house for not more than about $ 25,000 which, at that time, was a pretty fair price for a three bedroom house.

I was pleasantly surprised by the friendliness and helpfulness of the real estate agent I approached. After learning a little bit about us and our situation he took me for a drive to southern part of Hayward to show me a house.

Boy, I liked it right away just seeing it from outside It sat in a middle of a nice wide and sloped street, just under the hills on the eastern side of Mission Boulevard. The owners were very friendly showing me the house with three bedrooms, living room with a fireplace, two bathrooms, double garage and covered patio leading to a small yard with a rhododendron and a large tree in it. In discussion with the real estate agent, they even agreed on an FHA loan, just "to help us to get into a house" as they put it. They themselves were moving just a couple of blocks away, a little bit higher to have a better view.

The next day I took Marta to see the house. She, too liked it! We drove around a bit and did find a small shopping center in the walking distance. Just a few blocks away was nice elementary school, just perfect for Milena to walk to.

We decided to start serious negotiations. The asking price of $ 30,000 was a little bit over our possibilities. The owners agreed to go down to $ 28,500 and we accepted. To get a mortgage we would have to have an income 4x higher than our monthly mortgage and property taxes payment of $ 250.- would be. Well, Marta and I combined didn't make $ 1,000 a month. I was earning $ 2.40/hr and even so I was working 60 hours a week we would only make some $ 700 a month, a far cry from the needed minimum. To overcome the gap, I went to Mr. T. and he agreed to write a statement for the mortgage company showing my earnings much higher.

I remember when the mortgage company representative came to see us and I told him that we would like to get the house, but are little afraid of getting such a burden on ourselves, he said: "Don't be afraid at all! Look at me, I came here five years ago without anything and now I have $ 200,000 in my savings!"

So it happened that we have gotten the mortgage and at the beginning of November 1971 moved into our own house at 628 Tina Way in Hayward. As a gift Mr. T. donated to us enough of very nice heavy woolen yarn to make carpets to fit the whole house. This yarn was originally ordered by Mary Tayler Moore in a deep, dark green color. For some reason she changed her mind and ordered different color from us, so the original yarn was available. We would pay just for making the carpets. Marta arranged with her boss Joe Franco to have our carpets made there. His son Mike did a very nice job weaving and installing our carpets. They were made as a shag, so it was like living on a large, lush meadow.

We felt like being on the top of the world!

Our good feelings came to a pretty severe crash when Milena and I went to her new school. It just happened that the school in our neighborhood was not for kids from our street! Milena had to be bused to Union City some 4 miles away!

Then, when the first rain came in December, we found out that the roof of our new home leaked. Now this was a real disaster, since we did not have money to fix it.

Fortunately, we moved into a really friendly place. As soon as we moved in Michael and Angela from across the street came to welcome us into the neighborhood. The same did people from the houses beside us. Michael suggested to contact the real estate man and complain about the roof. I did complain, and the real estate man did send a man to repair it!

Marta, as the good housekeeper started to clean the house from the bottom up and all around. Fortunately, the light fixtures and drapes came with the house, so after bringing in our few belongings, we were content in the half empty place. I was "commissioned" to paint the whole house. Marta liked all walls to be white, but Milena wanted her room to be painted apple green, of all colors. Our persuasion for not to do that was not accepted, so I gave up and fulfill her wish. To soften up the green monster I created some wall designs, like a large tree on the main wall over Milena's bed. After many years later Milena confessed, that she hated that color, but didn't want us to have the satisfaction of being right, so she lived with it for many years.

Oh yes, I remember those puppy years of my own life......

I also set up to make few things for the house. I was able to get an older work bench from Mr. T. and put it in the garage together with some basic tools I bought on sale. With little imagination I created (very nice I have to say) head boards for Milena's and our beds (we are still using ours up to now), converted the closet in the third bedroom into an open space shelf for books, knick-knacks and the TV set. We changed the whole room into a family room by opening wall leading to our living room. It was Marta's idea, and a very good one as we created a large everyday living space. By installing wooden folding doors, we even maintained a secluded space for eventual visitors to sleep in.

Another project I did was wooden wall coat hanger by the entrance door and few other decorating items made of wooden lattices. Yes, we were getting homey.

Milena liked her school and was getting very good grades that made us happy. Marta and I visited the school and talked to Milena's teacher who also impressed us very positively. Everything seemed to be in order. We did not like the way Milena would do her home works, though. The finished papers she would just fold and put in her pants back pocket. She said that that was the norm and everybody was doing it. That didn't go well with our Czech upbringing, where school was very highly regarded institution and a place of pretty strict discipline. When, at the end of her school year Milena brought her report card full of As and Bs, we were happy until we found out that they did not finish any of the books in any of her subjects. I tried to finish at least the math with her, but it was difficult, because Milena felt that I was just overdoing it.

When we talked with our neighbors and complained about Milena's school, one of them suggested to send her to the private Catholic school near-by. His daughter attended it also and he was happy with it. He even suggested helping us to enroll Milena for the next year there. Marta and I talked it over and decided that the extra money would be worth it even if we would have to economize a little more.

It was the Saint Clements Junior High Milena started the new school year in. She did not like it, especially to wear the school uniform and the much stricter regiment there. Her marks were not as good as those at the state school, but she was learning much more! Eventually she made friends there and was content with the situation. There was another benefit to her attending the Saint Clements. After graduating from it she was eligible to go straight to the Moreau Catholic High School, one of the best schools in Alameda County, sitting just beside the Saint Clements. We are sure that our decision was a correct one and helped Milena a lot in her future life. To our surprise and delight she later even acknowledged that to us.

Marta didn't like the look of linoleum in her kitchen, so we decided to replace it with floor tiles. After inquiring about the price, I decided that I will do it myself, even that I have never done anything like that before. I bought some Do It Yourself books, we selected nice, double fired narrow tiles, and after few mistakes (that I corrected) I tiled the kitchen and both bathrooms on top of it. After almost forty years all the floors still look like new......

It confirmed the old saying that one can do whatever one wants if only one tries hard enough.

Our lives settled down. Every chance we got we would still take trips to our near and far surroundings. In our neighborhood there was a large public swimming pool whose membership we were able to buy for a discount from an outgoing member. Milena and her friends, whose families were also members, loved to go there to swim and meet other young people. Eventually Milena ended on the club swim team and was performing quite well. Her only complaint was that her beautiful long blond hair always turned green due to the chlorine in pool.

Milena's school required more of our time transporting her to and fro, so Marta, after long deliberation, decided to learn how to drive. I was happy to take that task, and in course of few Sundays taught Marta how to master that four wheel beast.

It was time to buy the second car. After spending few days prowling the used car lots alongside Mission Boulevard, I came across a white, eight-cylinder Matador, that we got for $ 2,000 at the end of 1973. The air-conditioning in it made our trips much more enjoyable, especially in the hot summer days. Marta liked that "monster", as she put it, which made it much easier on me and my family transportation duties.

All this time I was still working on the night shift, usually from noon to midnight, so jus about everything concerning Milena's upbringing and our household fell squarely on Marta's shoulders.

Well, she definitely did a very good job of everything. I am sure it wasn't an easy street all the time.

Another very important event in our lives occurred. At the beginning of May 1975, we were all invited for our citizenship examination. We studied all the materials very hard, passed the examinations and after swearing in we became full U.S. citizens! Our new lives started in earnest.

Miroslav Kolias

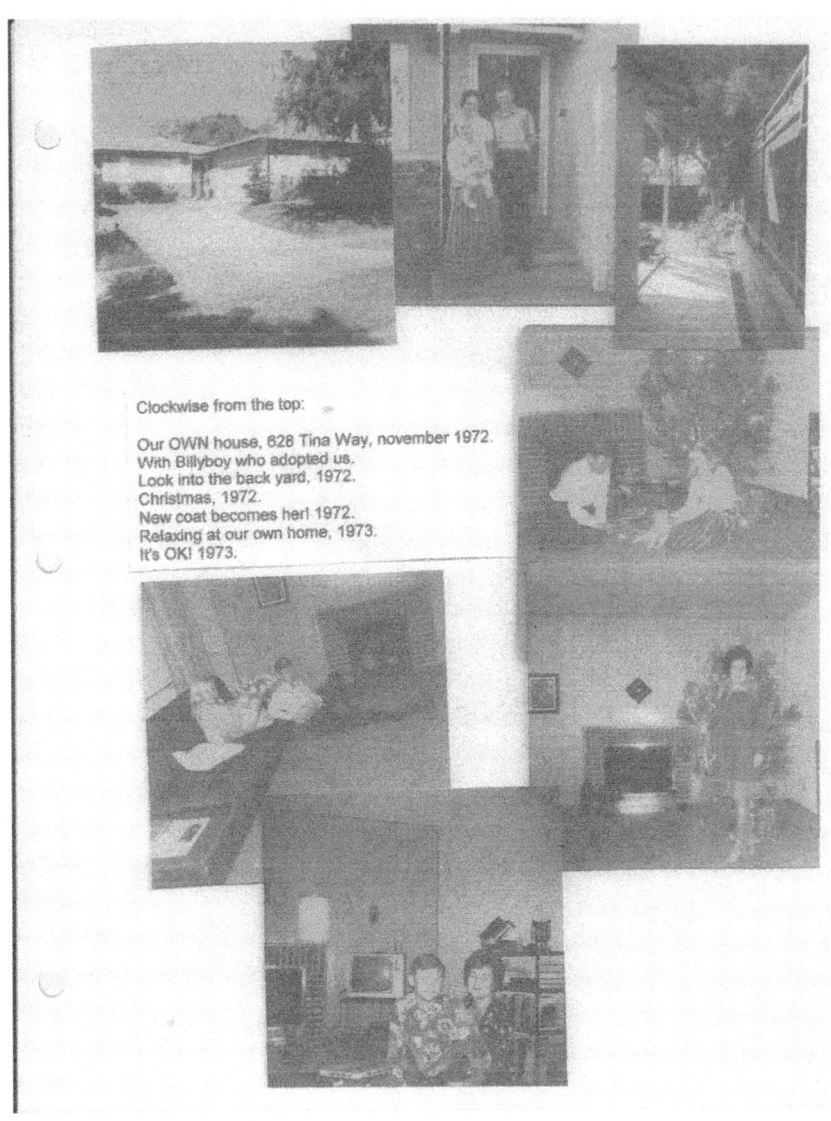

Clockwise from the top:

Our OWN house, 628 Tina Way, november 1972.
With Billyboy who adopted us.
Look into the back yard, 1972.
Christmas, 1972.
New coat becomes her! 1972.
Relaxing at our own home, 1973.
It's OK! 1973.

Building our future.

In May of 1975 my father came for a visit. It was a big deal, because to get out of the Communist Czechoslovakia, and especially when your children lived in a capitalist country, was not a simple task. We have sent a visit invitation for both, my mom and my dad, but my mom refused to come. She still did not approve of our leaving the country, the patriot she always was. In the invitation we would have to guarantee that we would completely take care of the visitor, his room and board and any eventual medical expenses and care. On the top of it we would have to purchase his air tickets (to which Mr. T. actually contributed), because firstly he would not have the means and secondly his country would not release foreign currency for such a "trivial" cause.

Anyway, my dad came to Oakland flying from Zurich, Switzerland and we had to live through some tens moments when his plane couldn't touch the tarmac correctly and had to go up and try again, actually two times! Probably some novice pilot was sweating in the cockpit.

My father was trying to learn English from a book for this occasion, but to be sure I wrote him few simple phrases needed in airports and on the plane in Czech and English, so he would be able to manage changing planes in Zurich and the trip to California.

It was an emotional moment when we all met after the long six years.

The whole trip was supposed to last three months in which my father was also to go to Canada to see Pavel and his family for a month. We had a great time with him, traveling around, even to Oregon and Nevada. My dad loved everything about his trip, but when asking him what made the greatest impression on him, he replied: "Well, all those old ladies behind the wheels of those huge automobiles"! He never learned how to drive a car. To own a car back home was practically impossible for us anyway.

After a month my dad set for trip to Canada. Again, I wrote him all the necessary phrases. He enjoyed his trip to Truro, Nova Scotia to see Pavel and his family tremendously, but on his returning trip back he had to change planes in Toronto coming from Halifax, Nova Scotia and then again in Chicago. Well, he thought that he already knows enough of the language to try on his own. We were all waiting in San Francisco for his plane, but when it arrived, there was no dad on board! After asking questions, the officials got quite concerned, because, when purchasing his tickets to Canada, we stipulated that he does not speak English and that he needs assistance changing planes.

Many phone calls ensued and, finally, they were able to locate him still in Toronto! Apologies and promises abounded. He was going to come the next day for sure.

When he finally came out of the plane, we thought that he would be all crushed by the terrible experience, but he came out all smiles!

"They took me to Chicago," he said "and because there was no connecting flight to San Francisco they put me into Hilton for the night and even fed me a dinner! Now, how otherwise I would be able to sleep in Hilton of all places?"

Never mind all our worries, he became a true world traveler!

In the next years my father would come to see us here two more times. On his second visit he confessed that only now he can really enjoy everything, that the first one was just a constant blur of so many to him strange and different things.

The next year in April I arranged for some free time from work and we decided to go and see Pavel in Canada. We flew to Detroit, rented a car and drove across the border to Windsor, Canada to visit our friends Liba and Pepa who came there via Italy where their son Patrick was born. We couldn't stop talking about theirs and our immigration experiences. Their way out was much more colorful than ours. Liba was pregnant, they didn't know Italian at all, were living in horrible refugee camp (something like we did for a short time in Traiskirchen), had to go to the hospital for Patrick's delivery and finally were able to immigrate to Canada. Pepa, an engineer, after getting a language schooling like Pavel and Lida did, got a good job with a company manufacturing vinyl capsules to be filled with various drugs. Eventually he practically was running the company, after many years, of course.

Anyway, after so very nice welcome and spending couple of days with them, we continued to Toronto, where the people from Krasna Lipa to whom we sent the "invitation" letter from Austria lived. After another very nice day with them we continued to spectacular Niagara Falls, further alongside the St. Lawrence River to Montreal for the night and a visit to the Olympic Stadium there. Crossed back to the US and through Bangor, Maine the next day we continued in the north-east direction (and with Milena driving part of the way) back to Canada's New Brunswick province and finally to Truro, Nova Scotia.

I still remember parking our car in front of Pavel and Lida's house and after sounding our horn how Pavel came out of the house, running and screaming with delight to welcome us all with his outstretched arms. Pavel and I felt into a strong and long embrace, screaming and crying at the same time.

It's needless to say that it was a fantastic get-together, five wonderful days with Pavel's family. We loved his kids, whom we never had a chance to meet before, Vera and Greg. Vera, beautiful blond girl was born, unbelievably on the same day as Milena, only ten years later and Greg was a strong loveable baby. Lida was a perfect hostess, and we liked their two-story house sitting in the suburbs on a large grassy lawn with a vegetable garden in the back.

Pavel took us to see the dye house he worked for, much greater and larger affair than the one I was working in. I was very proud of him, running such a large mill after such a short time. Pavel and Lida introduced us to all kinds of people and showed us Halifax, their capital and many other interesting places. It was a great visit!

Unfortunately, it was time for us to depart for our journey back.

Heading south we entered the US again and continued alongside the Atlantic coast (so much different than our Pacific coast) all the way to Boston and New York. I found driving in New York a total nightmare, gone was our West Coast easy going driving. To me the drivers in New York were just crazy.

Nevertheless we managed to drive through Manhattan, went to see the Statue of Liberty, all the way up into her torch, had a lunch in a Captain's Club close to the Battery Park (I still remember that a side salad consisting of two small pieces of tomato and one piece of lettuce costed us as much as the whole dinner back home) and managed to get through a tunnel into New Jersey to visit Marta's cousin Dolfi and her family in Eatontown. Dolfi as a little girl with her

JUST ANOTHER ORDINARY LIFE

family had to leave Czechoslovakia after the war for Germany. There she met an US soldier, married him and came with him to "America".

The next day we started east again and drove the beautiful countryside through Appalachian Mountains to Pittsburgh to visit other friends we knew from the Austrian refugee camp. We wanted to bring them a flower bouquet, so we stopped in a store to get one. Standing in line to pay, Milena came to Marta and showed her a $ 20 bill she just found on the floor. Marta explained to her that we are in pretty poor part of the city, and that she should give the money to the cashier with the explanation that she just found it there. At that time, it was quite a large sum, and some not very well-to-do family could really miss it. Milena did just that, but later she told us that she felt quite stupid doing it as she thought that the cashier would just pocket the money anyway.....

Another very nice welcome at the Hromulak family awaited us. They both worked for a large department store and were able to buy a nice house in which they raised their three children Ivo, Jana and Petr.

The following day our car took the eastern direction again all the way to Cleveland and to see yet another friends from Austria, the Kacr family. Ota and Daja bought a small clothes cleaning establishment where they slaved from morning to dawn every day. Ota was cleaning and pressing, Daja had a sewing machine and would do the alterations for their customers on it. Marta and I never saw anyone working so hard as they did. Their son Otik took Milena for the night on the town and Ota and Daja took us to a nice dinner on the top of one of the skyscrapers overlooking the rivers confluence.

Next morning found us on our way back to Detroit again. The whole trip was a fantastic and unforgettable one.

It was the last long trip we had as a family. Milena was growing fast into a beautiful young lady, so it was no surprise that she started to date. Marta and I tried to talk her from doing that, but with not much success.

So it happened that one day she brought to introduce a young man, Tony Rago, about four years her senior to us. Tony was from a local family. His father, also Tony, of Italian descent was working as a glass blower for a sign company. Tony's mother Elsie came from a German stock and was tending to their immaculate house. Tony, being the baby of the family, after High School graduation, learned how to blow glass from his father and was working for the same company also.

Marta and I liked Tony, but we felt that they should take it slowly. Well, it's easier said than done, I guess. After all I still remembered my own youth.....

Tony's family lived close-by so we became friends with his parents. His two sisters Anna, a teacher and Pamela, a sales lady were already married and living in their own places.

It didn't take long, and in the spring of 1977 Milena and Tony came to tell us that they'd like to get married. Tony bought a nice apartment in Fremont and was starting his own sign business after he lost his job.

How that happened was that he just learned how to blow swans from a glass tube. Proudly, on his break time, he went to the office showing his mastery to the ladies there. His boss suddenly walked in, and seeing Tony there, started to bully him and ordering him to get his ass out of there! Well, Tony punched him in the nose! No need to say that he lost his job immediately.

Tony's new company The Rago Neon was already getting nice orders so Tony was very positive about the future of his business.

For us it was quite a disappointment, because I was not able to get regular higher education and with Marta, we were hoping that leaving the Communist country Milena will be able to achieve that and enrich her life. Another problem for the wedding was that we just bought a small rental house and had spent all our money on it. The rent there actually did not pay the mortgage, because we only had a minimum down payment. Being raised in totally different environment and not having supporting family around, we just couldn't see ourselves to get into a debt any further. We explained that to Milena and Tony and they didn't want to wait and rather agreed on a small, in the court wedding consisting of only the immediate family members.

Tony's shop was in Fremont and I remember going there and help Tony with installation of some work benches. I liked Tony a lot, he was a hard working, neat man, good professional and an Eagle Scout to guarantee his character.

After some deliberations Marta and I agreed to give them our blessing. After all we came here in large part to ensure Milena a good future, so if Tony was the choice to spent her life with, we were happy for her.

And so it happened that on June 17th 1977 our small group gathered in the Hayward courtroom to witness Tony and Milena's vows.

The courtroom was packed with all kinds of people awaiting their turns before the presiding judge. Obviously, he didn't want the young couple waiting through the sordid accusations, pleas and defenses he had on his calendar and took Tony and Milena as his first case. The judge had a nice speech about the commitments they are about to enter into and sound suggestions for their relationship and life together. After that he asked them the most important question and receiving the sound "I do!" from both of them and pronounced them man and wife.

After the ceremony we all went into a nice park in Castro Valley where our photographer was already waiting to take pictures of the happy couple and all of us together.

It was a nice sunny day, Tony looked handsome and mature in his suit and Milena felt good in her simple dress, high heels and a bouquet of flowers in her hands. Marta and I, Elsie and Tony, Anna and Bruce, Pamela and Bob and the Michalek's wished them again all the best, after which we all went to San Mateo for an official wedding lunch.

The food was excellent, the party was happy and even the chef came to congratulate Tony and Milena, who soon after that left to Los Angeles for their honeymoon.

About a month later Elsie arranged for a large, very nice party for the whole Rago family to celebrate Milena and Tony's marriage. So, Marta and I were able to meet everybody and we were happy that Milena is going to be a part of such a nice group of people.

To end all this, I am happy to say that both, Tony and Milena stuck to their promises to each other and that they are, despite some few early tough times, still happily married, raising their two wonderful children and tending to their quite a bit larger business until now, some thirty two years later.

JUST ANOTHER ORDINARY LIFE

Clockwise from the top:

Trip to see Pavel's family, 1976.
Vera, Greg, Pavel at Peggy's Cove, Nova Scotia, Canada.
Marta with Lida.
Pavel's back yard.
Exactly ten years apart!
Don't they look like sisters?
To the Statue of Liberty.

Miroslav Kolias

HAYWARD JUNE 17th 1977

Thirteen people at the wedding and the marriage is still going strong! Standing: Draha Michalek, Eva Michalek, Zdena Michalek, myself, Bob and Pamela Accardo, Anna Andrade, Tony Rago, Bruce Andrade. Sitting: Tony, Milena, Marta, Elsie Rago.

Clockwise from the top:
Milena and Tony on our back yard, 1979.
Our 20th Anniversary, Carmel 1978.
We've got beautiful present from Voitre Marek in Australia, 1980.
Christmas 1980 at our place.
Milena with Eva Michalek and Gigi, 1973.

Miroslav Kolias

Milena and Tony's trip to Czech, 1984.
Front row: Milena, Jirka, Mirek.
Middle row: Jirka, Pavel, Petr, Mirek.
Back row: Michal, Maruska, Jana, Bohunka, Vlastik.
Pavel and Petr are Vlastik and Bohunka's kids.
Jana and Mirek are Mirek and Jaruska's kids.
Jaruska is missing in this group.
With Elsie on the airport.
With mom and dad in Krasna Lipa.

Miroslav Kolias

Moving on......

Suddenly our house felt empty.

Milena took her room furniture with her to their nice condo in Fremont Tony bought not too long ago. The newlyweds started to live their own life together and Marta and I felt like orphans, like people suddenly without a purpose in their lives.

This feeling didn't last too long, though. For some time, we left Milena's room empty just in case something would not get right in their marriage and she would want to come back to live with us again. We knew that Milena was not the easiest person to get along with, and that Tony will have to make many adjustments to assure successful continuation of their journey together.

Everything seemed to be on the up and up with them, though, so we started to change our lives in the direction of living together just by ourselves. I was still working the night shift and all those long hours, but every chance we got we would try to amuse each other. Marta expressed a desire to go and drive to the Canadian Rockies via Vancouver, and I was all for it.

It was one of the nicest trips we made together. The sheer vastness of the country we explored, the breathtaking vistas of mountains, woods and lakes we saw was just the right medicine to carry us into our new lifestyle.

The house did not feel empty anymore! We realized that we have done our life's duty, we raised our child to our best possibilities and now it was time to start living for ourselves. I have to say that Marta and I have had a good life together so far and we intended to continue in the same fashion, and I am happy to report that, until now, we are fulfilling our promise we gave each other quite well.

All I wrote so far was primarily for Milena and our grandchildren, so they would know where they came from on our side of the family. Now it's up to Milena and Tony to continue in the started good path.

After few years into their marriage Marta and I took Milena and Tony back to Czechoslovakia for Tony to meet our family there and at the same time introduce to them Tony as a new member of same. I think that this re-introduction was very successful on both sides. Unfortunately, Tony and I had to leave after just a week there, but Marta had a good chance to spent three more weeks with Milena traveling and visiting everybody there.

I still remember Marta telling me that Milena told her: "Mom, I feel like I belong here!"

In almost thirty years since that a lot changed in our lives. My Father passed on, my brother Pavel, who moved to California from Nova Scotia with his whole family, got killed in a car accident in Los Angeles where he worked. Our sister-in-law Lida, after Pavel's passing, moved from the very nice house they bought in Pinole to a condo in Hercules, where she lives with her son Greg until the present time. Vera graduated from College with two Master degrees, got married and later divorced. At the present time she lives along on the east coast doing a great job as a city planner. We didn't see my Grandma Marek anymore as she passed on before we were able to come to visit, my Aunt Bozka and Uncle Victor are not with us as well as are Uncle Pepa, Aunt Boza and Aunt Ella from Novy Bor.

It is not a simple thing to leave one's family behind forever. When one is young, and wants to explore world for whatever reason, he does not realize that. Only later in life he starts missing the old and familiar faces he grew up with, especially when he cannot go and see them any time he wants. When we were leaving our homeland, we did so with the understanding that we, most likely, will never be able to come back. Fortunately, times changed for better, the brutal Communist regime eventually collapsed and our old world became reachable again.

We were fortunate enough that we could invite many family members on mine and Marta's side over repeatedly, and we, too, were able to travel back home many, many times. My Mom is still living happily in her very nice retirement home, calling us daily over her phone, even several times a day. Her mind is clear and she thinks fondly about her four trips to see us all here in California.

Even though, when we left Czechoslovakia, my Mom said that she is not going to come to see us ever here, after the most joyful events in our and Milena's lives occurred - the births of our grandson Tony (Oh, another Tony??) and granddaughter Amanda- my Mom softened her stance and came for visits, first time when she was eighty five years young.

Our lives, after waiting twenty (!) years have changed by those two glorious babies again. The family continuity assured Marta and I offered help with our grandchildren which Milena happily accepted. I still hear her complaining: "Mom, nobody told me that having children is so much work!"

By then, being sixty, I retired from my work when I started to have some problems with my asthma I developed and my intestines which protested about all those chemicals I constantly was working with. Marta retired even earlier when Mr. T. sold the dye house, and the new owner offered me very substantial raise to assure my staying and running it as a VP of productions. I lasted for another ten years. When I started working there, we did about five jobs daily. When I retired, we frequently turned out seventy jobs a day.

Marta and I would take care of Tony almost entirely for his first three years. After Mandy was born, we would take partial care of her as well. When Tony started preschool, our involvement with the grandchildren became limited to a degree, but we are still in play with just about anything that is happening in Milena and Tony's family.

We also have a very good relationship with everybody in Tony's family, and that is great!

Well, I guess that's about all I wanted to say about our past, and can only wish for the good fortune and a long, happy and healthy lives for all of us!

Very happy Tony and Milena on the 15th of September 1997. After 20 years of waiting, little Tony was born!

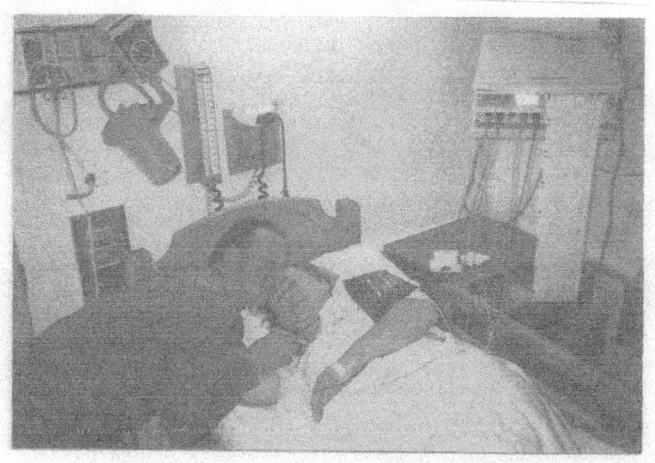

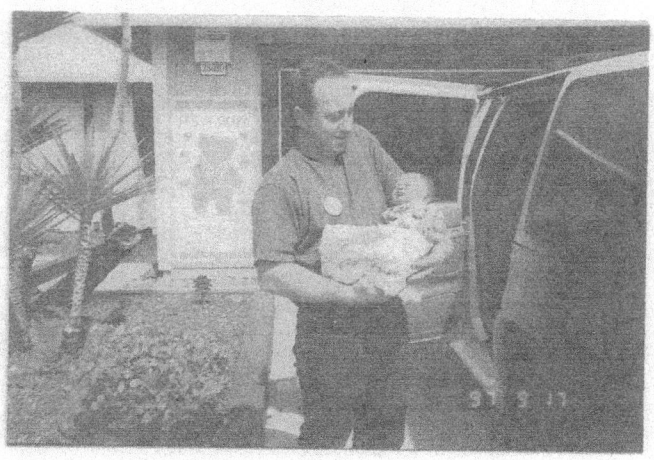

Miroslav Kolias

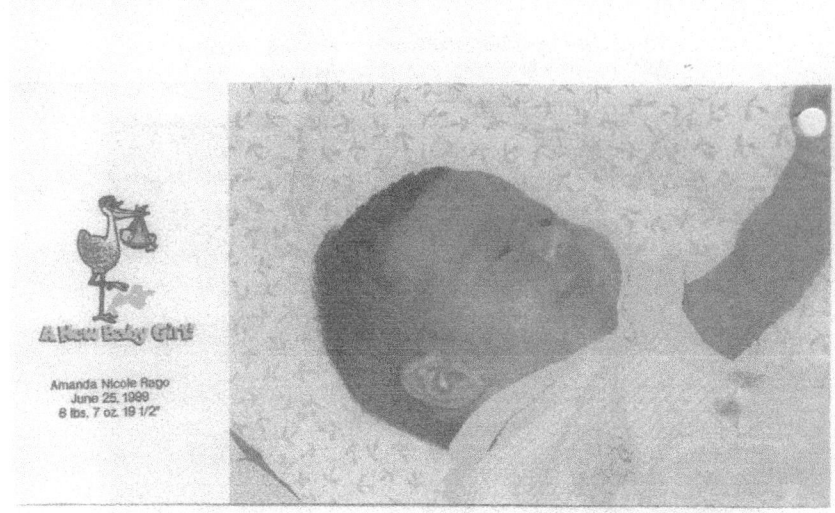

Hey, Tony, it's your little sister! Be very nice to her!

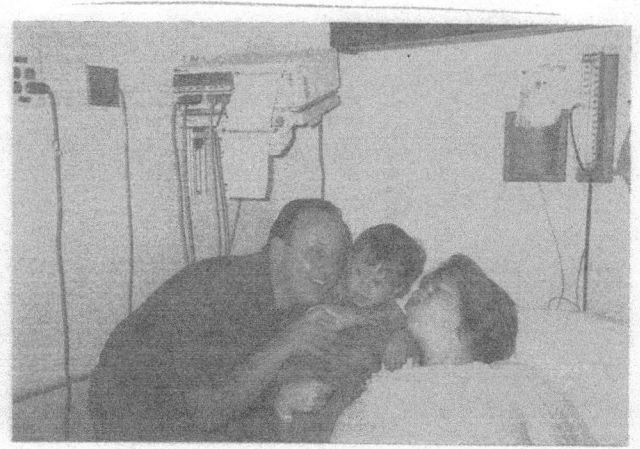

Epilogue.

The other day Marta and I drove across the San Mateo bridge, over the hills down to Half Moon Bay and continued north along the shore enjoying the breathtaking vistas along the way to Pacifica as we did many, many times before.

Stop at the local McDonald's for a cup of coffee and cookies (oatmeal for Marta and chocolate chips for me) is a part of this beloved trip. After that we would park at the Breakaway beach facing the swells and on the rocky cliffs breaking up waves spraying everything around with gazillion sunshine reflecting droplets of water and foam. We would roll down our windows and listen to the constant and yet always different, almost threatening sounds of the Pacific. I often would lower the back of my seat, close my eyes and drift into pleasant nap only being awaken by Marta in few minutes with offering of a small square of dark Ghirardelli chocolate. A leisurely stroll around the beach would follow before returning back home for lunch.

Yes, we are happy with our life and are content with the twists and turns it took. In few days we will both be 74, still being able to enjoy fully our extended family, even helping our growing grandchildren with their school work and the usual daily problems that seem so terrible to them.

Unfortunately, Pavel cannot do the same with his family, he would have richly deserved that. I am glad that we are in pretty close touch with them.

My mom is still alive, presently in the hospital, though, as she broke her leg going to her refrigerator for a snack. I do talk to her every day on the phone and am looking forward to see her up and around in July when with Milena and Mandy will travel together to the Czech Republic, just as we did three years ago with little Tony to show them where we did come from.

Leaving Czechoslovakia, we left everything behind. Our possessions and most importantly our families and friends, our history and our memories. We thought that we would not be able to come back, ever. Fortunately, this country welcomed us in and enabled us to build a new and happy life here. We made a lot of very good friends around us and are feeling completely at home. We are very grateful for that.

It took me over three years to put this "ordinary life" together, but please remember that English is still only my second language.

The life goes on and we do wish the best to all dear people we came in touch with during our journey through it.

Take a good care of yourselves and enjoy life as we did and do!

Marta's last days

Marta was a remarkable human being.

Happy, friendly, helpful, completely trustworthy.

She was the base rock of our family, guiding us well through the many difficult parts of our lives. She made friends easily, complete opposite of me, that was a big help to all of us, starting our new future here. She knew how to overcome difficulties. When we first came here, she would cry every day for three months, but never in front of Milena. Everything was so different from what we were used to, but gradually she started to like it and helped to build our good future.

Marta was in a pretty good health. She did suffer with arthritis for the last few years, though. Her mornings. Before she started moving for real, were the worst. Despite that, we would be walking every day for couple of miles through our neighborhood or alongside the beach in Pacifica, which she loved.

Marta was not in a hospital since Milena was born, save for a very short stay two months after that, to get her tonsils removed.

In the mid of December 2015, she started to complain about loosing her appetite, though. She went to see her physician, which she would do anyway about two times a year, and told him about that. After checking her vital signs and knowing her age, he advised her: "Well, if you don't like something, just don't eat it!". Unfortunately, he did not do or order any more thorough examinations.

The Christmas dinner at Milena's went just fine, Marta ate everything without a problem, as well as at the New Year's one.

On January 17th she did not feel well at all, so I took her to Emergency at San Leandro Kaiser hospital. After thorough examinations, they kept her over night and released her, but made an appointment for her on the 21st for an MRI, which she took.

Cancer of her pancreas was discovered.

The meeting with surgeon followed, who told her, that she is lucky, one of only 30% of patients with pancreatic cancer, who is good for a surgery, as, usually, this type of cancer is discovered too late, and people after that live 4-6 months only! Marta's cancer is just at the beginning stage.

A nurse there told us, that there are only three surgeons in Northern California, who do this type of surgery, and that the Marta's one is the best, and that she will let us know, when to go for the surgery.

On January 24th she was happy, talking with our neighbor Angela outside, and I joined them. Suddenly I noticed, that her eyes were turning yellow. Her skin, too, started to look a little bit yellowish.

We went to emergency again. This time they sent her up into the hospital room for observation and more examinations. The next day she was told, that they are trying to find the fastest day for her surgery.

Marta actually did not want to have one. She knew what this cancer meant. Milena and I talked to her and persuaded her that, since it's only at the beginning, there is a very good chance to be helped and live normal life after. Finally, Marta agreed to the surgery, which was supposed to be done in the Oakland hospital, but made it clear to all of us, and the surgeon, that, in case her heart would not take the surgery, or after the surgery, she does not want to be resuscitated.

While waiting for the surgery, I visited her for the first two days for a whole day, while she was also getting a lot of visitors wishing her nothing, but the best. Starting on her third day there, I would stay over night in her room, sleeping on the sofa there. It was a very nice private room with bathroom and a shower in it. Milena or Tony would be coming for several hours during the day, too. I would walk with Marta in the hall and would sing to her, just like when we were dating.

Since there was just a small ulcer at the end of the pancreas, but was preventing the important digestion juices to flow into her system, other surgeons tried two times, always by different means, in two days to open the way for them. It didn't work.

Finally, on the 3rd of February she was moved to Oakland for the main surgery, that was due the next day.

At nine next day Marta was taken to the surgery room. Milena and Tony were there with me. It is an awful time to be waiting for the result of such a difficult surgery, and hoping for the best. At about one o'clock her surgeon finally appeared, and gave us the bad news. Her cancer spread throughout the whole pancreas. He kept cutting small pieces of her pancreas and sending them to the lab for evaluation. After even the third piece came back positive, he decided to come out and see us. The only possibility was to remove the pancreas completely. What should he do?

We knew that Marta would have to be for the rest of her life on insulin, as the pancreas also controlled sugar in her blood, and testing herself all the time. Not a very good prospect, but surly better than not having Marta at all.

After a short discussion, we agreed with the removal.

Marta came out of the surgery at four o'clock in the afternoon.

Marta was moved to the recovery room, and I was allowed to go and be with her. She didn't know anything. After she came to, holding her hand, I tried to explain what happened.

She was familiar with it. She kept several medical books and dictionaries which she often would go through them, learning about different illnesses her friends would complain about.

After I told her I could see desperation in her eyes.

Finally, her surgeon came to see her, and was explaining the situation. It di not help Marta at all. She was depressed.

When moved back to her room, she was not able to sit or stand. She was hooked to many different wires and tubes, but, luckily, she did not feel any pain. I was keeping her company 24 hours, her room was similar to the one before, and Milena and Tony would stop by every day, too. Both kids came several times also, but I could see that Marta's situation disturbed them greatly.

Marta was making slow progress.

She started to eat a little, and was able to sit for a while, as spe4cial nurses would come, and help her move arms and legs. When different physicians would come to see her few times a day, Marta would always tell them: "Please, let me go!"

I will never forget that.

On the 16th of February Marta was able to stand up and make two steps! My eyes got wet, but I was happy as a lark!

She will make it!

In the morning of the 17th, she did not talk much, though. Before noon Tony and Milena came, but Marta hardly moved. We were sitting by the window and talking over the situation, when suddenly Marta started to breath heavily, and her heart rate went up to close of 200.

In about a second Marta stopped breathing completely!

I jumped up and started to compress Marta's chest, when suddenly realized that she didn't want to be helped, if something like this happened. I stopped, and with nurse, who came rushing in after Milena called her, and Milena and Tony watched silently as Marta passed on. What a sad, sad day.

It has been more than one and a half year since that awful day. I'm slowly getting used to living alone. Every day, unless I'd be away, which doesn't happen often, I would go or drive to Marta's niche by a beautiful copy of Michelangelo's Pieta, Marta's resting place. Milena is taking very good care of me, but I still think that Marta will walk into our room by any minute………

MARTA KOLIAS
August 8th 1935 - February 17th 2016

Marta was born in Moravia part of Czechoslovakia just before WW II from which her father never returned. The life with sister Olga and later also Dobruska for their mother was not easy then. Marta showed a lot of strength to go through high school and further studies to become a professional photographer, at which profession she did not work for too long, though.

After meeting her future husband for 58 years Mirek, she moved to Bohemia where their only child, daughter Milena, was born in 1960. Life in the Communist Czechoslovakia was not an easy one, so when the Soviet army occupied Czechoslovakia, they all managed to leave for Austria and after seven months of uncertainty in a refugee camp there, they all came to California in September of 1969.

Even without speaking English and being practically penniless, they started a new life together in which Marta was the leading part. In 1974 they all became US citizens. Marta made many very good friends here, raised Milena to be a smart and beautiful lady who married a young starting businessman, Tony Rago.

Marta was always the main pillar, the guiding light to Milena and her two children, who lovingly called Marta by the Czech expression for Grandma - Babi.

When retiring, Marta loved to travel, even across the US and back in 42 days with Mirek. They lived a happy, loving life just to about a month ago, when the sudden and unexpected disease struck.

After a very long and difficult surgery Marta fought hard for almost two weeks, but her heart did not co-operate, and with Mirek, Milena and Tony beside her, she died in the hospital.

She will be dearly missed by her extended family and many friends close and afar......

We will say good-bye to Marta at the Mission Chapel of the Chapel of the Chimes Mortuary in Hayward on Thursday, February the 25th at 10 AM.

Marta's wish was for instead of flowers to donate to St. Jude's Hospital.